D0594153

STAINED GLASS CRAFT

By
J. A. F. DIVINE, A.R.C.A.

Responsible Lecturer in Art, Department of Training for Teachers,
Loughborough College and Loughborough College Summer School

and

G. BLACHFORD, D.L.C.(Hons.)

Craft Master, The Wyggeston Grammar School for Boys, Leicester

With Frontispiece in Colour
and Ninety-Two Line Illustrations

FOREWORD BY
P. H. JOWETT

Dover Publications, Inc.
New York

Published in Canada by General Publishing Company, Ltd., 30 Lesmill Road, Don Mills, Toronto, Ontario.

Published in the United Kingdom by Constable and Company, Ltd., 10 Orange Street, London WC 2.

This Dover edition, first published in 1972, is an unabridged republication of the work originally published in 1940. It is reprinted by special arrangement with Frederick Warne & Company, publisher of the original edition.

International Standard Book Number: 0-486-22812-6
Library of Congress Catalog Card Number: 73-184692

Manufactured in the United States of America
Dover Publications, Inc.
180 Varick Street
New York, N. Y. 10014

FOREWORD

THE authors of this text-book have, I think wisely, concentrated their attention on craftsmanship, and in so doing have produced a work which should prove of real value to those who wish to obtain first hand knowledge of the problems involved in the making of a piece of stained glass.

The text is simple, direct, and easy to follow; the illustrations are extremely helpful and admirably explain the various processes. These processes are clearly described in a logical sequence which is excellently planned, and finally there is a chapter on stained glass as a school craft. This will, I hope, encourage many teachers to use this medium as a subject for craft teaching in schools, and to realize that, in its simpler forms, the craft of stained glass is quite within the scope of any school with a reasonably adequate craft room.

It is particularly encouraging at the present time to welcome this book, which deals with the permanent value of fine craftsmanship. It may be hoped that the thought and understanding that have gone to the making of it will inspire and help those who read it.

P. H. JOWETT.

CONTENTS

INTRODUCTION

THAT a very large proportion of people appreciate stained glass work is evident from those who find pleasure in examining specimens in churches and other buildings. There are, however, in contrast, very few who seem to realize that the work as a craft is within the scope of the home or school workshop. That such is a fact, it is the purpose of this book to inform and explain. Work in stained glass has its own utilitarian value, in addition to which it provides a practical background with which to study more clearly the beauty and merits of historic pieces. Furthermore, it provides a unique artistic experience.

Work in the arts and crafts brings its own particular non-material satisfactions, as those fortunate people with natural aptitudes for creation and appreciation fully realize. It is known also that the highest abilities and deepest satisfactions are brought about by a comprehensive training which includes work in as wide a variety of crafts as possible. The contribution to such a training offered by work in stained glass, which we have

INTRODUCTION

referred to as a unique experience, is the relation of the medium to light. The material used in this craft has, in addition to other characteristics, the quality of allowing light to pass through it from back to front instead of reflecting light back from the front as in the usual case of craft media. The variation of hue and intensity of the background light provides stained glass with a sparkling life which results from a combination of the natural qualities of man-made craftwork and the illumination of the changing colours of daylight.

This book sets out to indicate an inexpensive method of working in stained glass, particularly suited to home workshops and to schools. Windows and panels may easily be made with pieces of coloured glass cut to fit and leaded together to form some required shape. In addition there are other processes to which the fragments of glass may be subjected before leading together. These processes vary in their expense and demand of equipment but they include no insuperable difficulties. This book deals, in the beginning, with the construction of a simple window through all its stages. The book then continues by returning to a consideration of those intermediate processes which may be employed if windows of a more advanced character are to be attempted.

The whole value of the work in this craft, as

INTRODUCTION

in any, lies in the execution of purely original designs based upon the sound appreciation of the limitations, possibilities and qualities of a unique material.

STAINED GLASS CRAFT

CHAPTER I

AN OUTLINE OF THE CRAFT

THE material mainly used by workers in stained glass in window making is known as antique or pot metal glass. Other types, such as Flemish and cathedral, are used on account of their low price, but they have none of the interesting qualities that are to be found in the antiques. Although the actual manufacture of the glass does not directly concern us here, a visit to a glass works will be found both interesting and educational, and perhaps a brief account of the making will assist in the appreciation of the nature of the material.

Antique glass is obtained in comparatively small sheets about eighteen inches by two feet six inches. It is made by dipping a long tube into a molten mass of glass and collecting a lump on the end. This lump is formed into a bubble by blowing down the tube. A skilled glass blower can control most amazing shapes in this way, but

1

for the purposes of stained glass he is only required to produce a hollow cylinder, which he does by removing the ends of the elongated bubble.

While still plastic the cylinder is cut down one side and allowed to settle on a flat stone. In settling, the underside of the glass becomes relatively flat, including, however, any irregularities that may be present in the surface of the stone. The upper surface of the glass retains undulations from blowing which make interesting variations in the colour. When the sheets of antique glass are delivered it will be seen that the long edges are irregular and rounded, being cut in the plastic state, while the short edges are hard and sharp due to cutting when cold.

It is sometimes thought that the window designer is responsible for the actual colours of the glass but this, of course, is not so. The glass is manufactured in various colours which are produced by the inclusion of different metallic oxides in the molten mixture.

In some cases a lump of clear glass is taken up from a molten mass on the end of the tube and then dipped into another mass of coloured glass. When it is withdrawn it is covered with a coating of the coloured glass and, as the bubble is blown, this coating is spread out in the form of a very thin layer on the top of the clear glass. Glass having a thin layer of another coloured glass on it, is known as 'flashed'. Although the process is

2

usually practised with clear glass, combinations of coloured glass are not uncommon. Red glass is nearly always flashed, as a pure red glass would be very dark and would lose much of its transparency and translucency.

Many legends exist concerning the discovery of glass and it was known to the Egyptians as far back as 2000 B.C. Its use was also known to such early civilizations as the Assyrian, Phoenician, Etruscan, Greek and Roman. The first mention of the use of glass for windows, however, is in Lactantius (third century) and is also recorded by St. Jerome in A.D. 442. We believe the use of window glass was first introduced in Britain in A.D. 674 by Benedict Biscop. Examples of Anglo-Saxon glass have been found in places as widely separated as Faversham, Winchester and Castle Eden, while in the twelfth century a monk named Theophilus wrote a very full account of the stained glass industry. During the thirteenth century the industry became centred around Chiddingfold in Surrey. It was at this time that the art of working with stained glass reached its highest standard. In the fourteenth and fifteenth centuries began a decline that continued until the time of William Morris. This was due to the development of technique and the use of enamels which were employed to the detriment of the beauty of the natural characteristics of glass.

It is often supposed that present day glass makers are unable to produce the wonderful colours of the Middle Ages. Their present appearance, however, is due largely to the effects of time, and had they been seen when first put up their admirers would not have been so numerous. The pronounced effect of time is due to the fact that the chemical knowledge of that period was limited and only an inferior glass could be made. The colours used by the workers of the Middle Ages were limited in range and consisted largely of vicious reds and blues, while the basic ingredients of their glass included little more than 50% silica. This low silica content, compared with the 75% or so used to-day, resulted in a softer glass incapable of standing up to the acid attack of the atmosphere. It is this weakness that is alone responsible for the wonderful satin-like quality which can be seen in these old windows to-day. If examined closely the glass will be seen to have many minute holes, as well as filmy qualities which have been brought about by corrosion.

The worker in stained glass should study the development of the design of the craft from actual pieces whenever possible. The best styles and materials of early glass work are to be found in churches where the purpose of the window was to enrich the building, create emotion and depict scenes of Biblical history for the benefit of worshippers who could not read.

Some of the finest pieces of work, capable of producing great emotional reaction, are to be seen at Canterbury, York, Chartres in France and in Paris at Saint Chapelle. In the Victoria and Albert Museum, South Kensington, there is a valuable collection of glass work representative of many periods and styles.

CHAPTER II

It is felt that a brief survey of all the processes involved from the first rough sketch to the finished window will provide a clearer conception of the more detailed explanations set out in separate chapters. An appreciation of processes that lie ahead will greatly assist the worker during the earlier operations.

To construct a stained glass window or panel the following operations are involved:

1. **Design.** The design is first worked out on paper at a convenient size and proportion capable of being scaled up to the full size of the proposed window, and showing the general colour scheme.

2. **Cartoon.** The approved design is next enlarged. The enlargement is most likely effected by drawing, in which case care must be taken to see that the larger outline of the cartoon preserves the vitality of the small sketch. For speed and accuracy the small sketch is often enlarged to full size by photography, though this is not usually possible in the small workshop.

6

3. **Cutting.** A piece of tracing cloth or paper is spread over the cartoon and lines are drawn showing the size and shape of each individual piece of glass required to form the whole window. These lines are spaced to allow for the thickness of lead between the various pieces of glass. The tracing (called the cutline) is marked to show the colour of the glass required for each shape and all the pieces are then cut to size.

4. **Waxing Up.** When all the pieces are cut they are then placed on a large sheet of clear glass and secured in their correct positions by drops of beeswax (warmed to a molten state) at the corners. An even margin will separate all the units of glass and will represent the core of the lead.

Once the pieces have been secured the glass sheet may be fitted to an easel or frame and held up to the light to show the effect of the colours.

5. **Etching.** This process employs flashed glass, the thin top layer of which is etched away with hydrofluoric acid to reveal the base glass.

6. **Painting.** The painting of line work now takes place and the lines may be drawn directly on to the window as a whole, standing on the easel, or they may be drawn on the separate pieces removed from the frame and placed on the cartoon. The last method enables the worker to trace accurately the lines of the cartoon.

7. **Firing.** When the desired amount of pigment is added to the glass the separate pieces are placed in a kiln and fired to about 850°C. The firing operation fuses the pigment with the glass surface and renders the colouring permanent.

8. **Further Waxing Up and Painting.** After the first firing the glass is again waxed up into position and further painting is added.

The second painting is usually concerned with matting, stippling and other brushwork which supplements the already-fired line work. Should the first or second firing be in any way unsuccessful the glass may be touched up where necessary and given an additional firing.

9. **Staining.** Silver stain, if required, should be applied at this stage. It is generally painted on the back of the glass (See Fig. 71) and fired at a temperature somewhat lower than that required for opaque pigments. The result is a yellow colour varying from pale lemon to deep orange.

10. **Leading Up.** The separate pieces of glass are placed on a flat bench or board and joined together by strips of lead called 'calm'. (See Fig. 49.)

11. **Soldering.** The lead joints are cleaned and soldered. When all the joints on the top face of the window have been soldered it is carefully turned over and soldered on the reverse side.

12. **Cementing.** A cement of suitable constituents is brushed into the spaces between the lead and the glass. The leads are then pressed down neatly, cleaned, and the window left for the cement to dry.

13. **Fitting.** The finished work may be fitted to a window space and may require strengthening in some way. Alternatively the stained glass work may be in the form of a panel to be hung before a strong light and in this case it may be unframed, lightly framed in wood, or wire may be threaded round the outside leads and a loop made at the top for hanging.

CHAPTER III

DESIGN

DESIGN is of the greatest importance in any craft, and to those teachers or craftsmen who intend to use stained glass as a means of expression, the necessity for simplicity and severity cannot be too greatly emphasized. Much unsatisfactory work has been and is still being done where the beauty of the medium is lost because of unnatural liberties taken with the limitations of glass.

Design is a matter which usually provokes much criticism, and although one cannot formulate rules regarding it one must never strain the medium of a craft and hide the natural character of the material.

One cannot be dictatorial nor attempt to teach art, but clearly a sound practical knowledge of the technicalities of the craft and an ability to foresee the appearance of a design on paper as it will finally present itself in the finished work are necessary before we begin.

It has sometimes occurred that a painter has been asked to design a window and, having little or no knowledge of the craft, produces work of a nature quite foreign to the medium. Very often his design can only be adapted by great ingenuity on the part of the unfortunate craftsman who is expected to make the translation. Incidentally it is unusual at the present time to find a designer who completely executes his own design.

In many cases stained glass windows are produced by firms who are, perhaps naturally, primarily interested in the financial aspect of the industry, and the various processes of manufacture, including the design, become separated.

Some of the work involved in window production is almost entirely mechanical, for instance leading up, soldering, and cementing, but the designer should at least design his own glass shapes and do his own painting.

Before putting pencil to paper the designer should have three considerations clearly before him. These are the purpose which must be fulfilled when the window is in position, the decorative and constructive limitations of the materials, and finally the interesting arrangement of the shapes. Immediately the designer becomes sensitive to these considerations and to the special problems of the craftsman, his own difficulties increase. Supposing the designer is an accomplished figure draughtsman and is capable of producing interesting figure compositions, he is now confronted with the necessity of deciding how far he should allow the character of glass to interfere with the representation of natural forms. Experiment in the workshop shows that glass breaks in simple long angular shapes, that the surface is smooth for painting while the actual application of the pigment allows of such decorative treatments as scratching and stippling before firing. The discovery of these possibilities and the employment of the processes will greatly influence the work of the designer. He must decide whether the interest of his work will depend upon a clever imitation of natural forms or upon the creative sense which prompts him to seek to express himself within the limits imposed by glass.

The authors feel that the medium should be used primarily for its own sake, the arrangement of the glass and the qualities produced by the various techniques employed should be governed by the purpose for which the window is required. Realistic treatments of natural forms will most certainly detract from the character of the glass and should be avoided. The manner in which natural figures and forms must be conventionalized will be determined by the character of the material. Often the natural proportions will be distorted, both in shape and colour, to aid the interesting arrangement of the design as an expression in glass. The painting methods of the thirteenth century craftsmen should be studied for the rhythmic brushwork and conventional arrangements of hands and feet.

A study of heraldry is very useful in the development of a sense of decorative arrangement suitable for glass. The reason for this is that the problem of the ancient heraldic designer was similar to that of the designer in glass and, although the use of light is different, the need to avoid foreshortening is equally important for both purposes. The shield was originally designed as a distinguishing mark, easily read in battle. For this reason the formal heraldic charges evolved as simple decorative shapes that could be easily recognized.

These heraldic shields are very attractive because of their simple colours and the satisfying manner in which the shapes of the charges are conventionalized to fill the shield spaces.

When heraldry is applied to stained glass an additional problem arises from the fact that light falls on the back of and through the design and not from the same side as the observer as in the case of heraldic shields. The light coming from the back increases the difficulties of perspective in the design. Human figures lend themselves well to the proportions of tall windows and the traditional use of glass in churches has made figure work indispensable. Stained glass is not, however, a suitable medium for portraying ideas of distance or foreshortened figures, such as the front view of a man bending forward. This pose should be shown as a side view, as attempts at a front view would most likely result in peculiar effects not intended. The bending figure would, as likely as not, appear headless. Furthermore, a strong light from the back will considerably reduce the apparent thickness of black lines

painted, or lead, on the glass while areas of un-
painted glass surrounded by painting will appear
enlarged (Fig. 1). These considerations are
especially important when lettering is incor-
porated in the design.

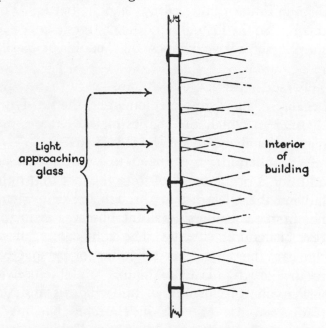

Fig. 1.—Section of window showing how light tends to lessen
lines of paint and leads as it penetrates window.

We have emphasized the necessity of expressing
the character of the medium in all designs. The
characteristic qualities of transparency and translucency insist that glass should be used in two-
dimensional compositions which depend for their
interest upon the colour pattern and the brilliancy
and sparkle of the light as it passes through the
window to the darker interior. It follows there-

fore that the choice and composition of colours is particularly important as therein the basis of an interesting design is laid. The selection and arrangement of the different coloured glass must be made by examining the specimens in the window position, i.e., with a strong light behind.

A useful introduction is to apply the heraldic law of blazon which disallows colour to be placed on colour or metal on metal. This need not be rigidly adhered to but will provide a basis for patterning dark glass on light and light on dark. In addition, the various shapes, which go together to form the whole window, must not run contrary to the character of glass. Shapes which are long and narrow are difficult to cut and fire, and make for weakness in the finished window. The position for the leads is of great importance, too, for they not only connect the glass components but, when well-designed, greatly strengthen the finished product. These last two points will be dealt with more fully in Chapter IV.

The designer who is conversant with his craft begins his work with a small sketch in pencil or ink, and then experiments with a colour scheme. The small sketch is coloured with water-colours and the outline may require repeating several times, with the use of tracing paper, to allow experiment with colour schemes. These small traced sketches enable the colour scheme to be criticized apart from the actual drawing.

When time and material are of little consequence an experienced glass worker may choose to build up a window with only the roughest of sketches. In this case he cuts and fits the glass as he goes along with no reference to definite cut lines. Such a method often produces very interesting results, but opportunities for experiment of this type rarely occur.

The chief points to bear in mind when designing a window are:

1. The shapes into which glass naturally breaks.
2. The effect of the penetration of light from back to front.
3. The various methods by which paint can be applied to the glass.

CHAPTER IV

CARTOON AND CUTLINE

As explained in Chapter II the preliminary sketch of the design should be correctly proportioned and therefore capable of being scaled up to full size without difficulty. The process of enlarging will no doubt be by some drawing method and the enlarged drawing may call for some modifications of the design which were less obvious in the small sketch. The full-size working drawing is termed the 'cartoon' and it should preserve as far as possible all the vigour and vitality of the small drawing.

The usual method of enlarging by drawing is by 'squaring up'. The frame of the small sketch is divided up into equal parts, and squares are drawn over the design. The full-size frame on the cartoon paper is similarly divided up into the same number and arrangement of relatively larger squares. The enlargement proceeds by reproducing the design square by square using proportionately larger measurements (Fig. 2). The medium for the cartoon may vary according to which the designer finds the most suitable for his own technique. The most usual forms are with

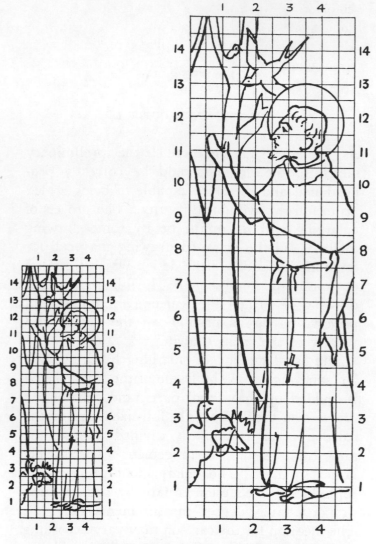

FIG. 2.—Method of enlarging by squaring up.

charcoal, pencil or water-colour. If water-colour is adopted, sepia or other strong tones should be used that are dark enough to show through the glass when it is placed on the drawing for tracing purposes. Special cartoon paper may be purchased in large rolls, or, alternatively,

FIG. 3.—Drawing with charcoal tied to stick.

several sheets of cartridge paper may be gummed together to meet the purpose.

The paper on which the cartoon is to be drawn

FIG. 4 (a).—Part of cartoon showing arrangement of leads.

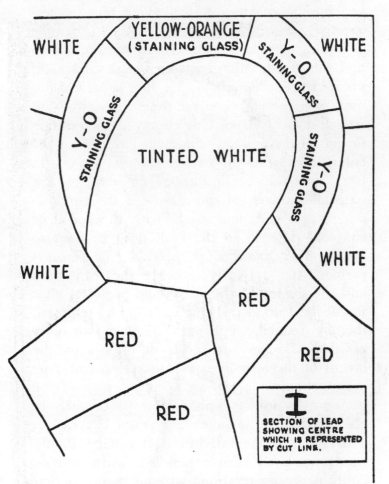

FIG. 4 (b).—Cutline. (Drawn on tracing paper or tracing cloth).

should be pinned up on the wall at a convenient height for working. In this way the drawing may be considered without distortions due to perspective.

The cartoon paper should now be squared up and the design enlarged from the small sketch, squared proportionately. Certain modifications may be necessary when the design is viewed full size in a vertical position closely corresponding to that of the finished window. Throughout the enlarged drawing the worker should continue to bear in mind the limitations enforced by the natural character of the glass. If the window-design is large a long stick, with the pencil or charcoal fastened to the end, may be used to obtain freer linework (Fig. 3). The finished cartoon should clearly indicate the lead lines, and the shapes for the individual pieces of glass should be true to the character of the material, thereby reducing cutting difficulties wherever possible. Designers in the trade often leave the layout of the lead lines to others, but the true design should include an accurate plan of the positions for leads. This applies particularly to glass craftsmen who have had no great experience. The layout for the individual glass shapes should be drawn finely with a pencil at first, and no doubt several alterations will be made so that colours and shapes may harmonize in the construction of a strongly built window.

When the cutline has been finally designed it should be traced on to tracing paper or cloth placed over the cartoon (Fig. 4). The traced cutline should be approximately $\frac{1}{16}''$ thick to represent the heart or core of the leads. The traced cutline shows up clearly if drawn in black Indian ink and it should follow the centre of the lead lines sketched on the cartoon.

The traced ink line may be drawn with a brush or, if it is found difficult to obtain an even line by this method, a ball-pointed pen may be

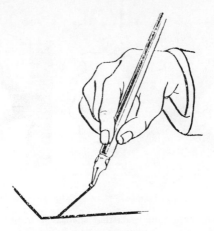

FIG. 5.—Ball-pointed pen.

employed (Fig. 5). When designing the cutlines for large windows horizontal leads should be carried through from side to side every nine or ten inches. These will form bars in the completed window which will greatly strengthen the large area of glass. This point will be dealt with more fully at a later stage. When making the cutline it should be borne in mind that, although varied thicknesses of leads may be used to help the quality of the window, these lines should not attempt to compete with the glass in the formation of the pattern.

Apart from considerations of strength and the avoidance of the lead lines competing with the glass pattern there are some other points to be observed. It is advisable to avoid crossing lead lines which will form a point of radiation in the design (Fig. 6). In addition to the worrying

FIG. 6.—Crossing leads.   FIG. 7.—Leads meeting at edge.

Arrangements of leads that should be avoided.

feature of such a radiation it is also a centre of weakness from the constructional viewpoint.

A similar feature to be avoided is the joining of two lead lines at the same point on the outside lead (Fig. 7). It has been stated that the lead lines should not compete with the glass shapes in the design of the window. Competition will be set up if the sweep of the lead lines, either by accident or intent, follows round the lines of figures or other objects of interest in the design and lead off to another part of the design (Fig. 8).

Sometimes it will be found impossible to avoid a few of these unfortunate features, in which case

FIG. 8.—Avoid leading too close to detail and continuing lead as shown at X.

the problem can be dealt with by concealing the weakness as much as possible by painting (Fig. 9).

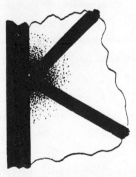

FIG. 9.—Matting or stippling glass to conceal awkward leading.

CHAPTER V

CUTTING THE GLASS

ALTHOUGH for some purposes a diamond cutter is the most efficient tool, a wheel cutter is more suited to the stained glass craft. The reason for this is that the curves and uneven surfaces of much of the glass used for this work prevent the cutting point of the diamond from making a clean continuous incision and the result is a jagged edge which makes for great difficulty in the process of leading-up. The wheel cutter should be chosen with care; the handle should fit the hand comfortably. Good quality wheels may be re-sharpened on an oilstone. Another important feature is that the design of the cutter should allow the worker to see his cut-line while cutting, thus ensuring cutting accuracy, which is the basis of the strength of the construction, a

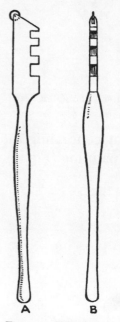

FIG. 10.—Wheel glass cutter. Note the three nibbling mouths of different sizes.

26

positive necessity where the window is being made to fill a definite position. Fig. 10 shows a well-designed wheel-cutter having a bevel in each side and a centrally-placed wheel. Incidentally the angle of these bevels is often parallel to the wheel bevel, a fact which greatly assists the workman in maintaining an accurate and constant angle when he is resharpening the tool on an oilstone. If desired the cutter bevels may be filed to match the wheel angle.

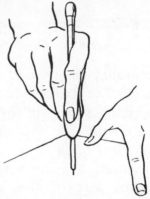

When cutting, the cutter is held between the first two fingers and steadied by the thumb and the third finger (Fig. 11). The glass should be held down firmly in position with the other hand. This position allows the cutter to be pushed or pulled freely.

FIG. 11.—Cutting the glass.

To make a cut the pressure should be lightly applied but constant, and the cutter must be held in a vertical position. One cut is quite sufficient, the cutting sound is quite characteristic, and on no account should the wheel be moved backwards and forwards across the glass, as in this way small cracks may be set up which will run and perhaps ruin a large piece of glass.

As mentioned in Chapter I, the two faces of the

glass will be found to vary considerably (Fig. 12). The cut is always made on the flatter or underneath surface, i.e., on the side of the glass which, when in a molten state, came into contact with the stone. Although this face is relatively flatter, it often includes ridges and other irregularities which have formed by contact with an imperfect stone. These irregularities may add a little difficulty to the cutting process but they do not interfere with the quality of the glass; in most

FIG. 12.—Showing section of antique glass.

cases they greatly add to the interest of the window. The flatter side of the glass always forms the inside surface of the window. Flashed glass is cut on the side opposite to the flashing, in this way the thin layer of coloured glass is always on the outside of the window. With practice the flashed side of the glass can be recognized instantly by glancing at the edge of the glass. If for some reason the flashed side is required on the inside the cutline must be reversed or a paper template of the shape made and turned over as a pattern.

The cutting bench should be solidly built and the top must be quite flat, of bare wood, or of wood covered with baize; in either case it will require levelling from time to time as most timber has a tendency to shrink and perhaps warp. Plate glass makes a fine bench top but is a more expensive item. When cutting dark glass it is necessary to have a light of some kind beneath the glass and the tracing. Fig. 13 shows a cutting bench built for this purpose.

Before commencing to cut, the shapes required should be carefully considered in relation to the glass sheet, for much glass may be saved by the

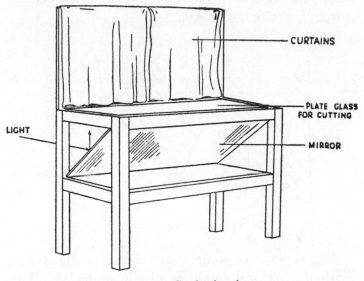

CURTAINS

PLATE GLASS FOR CUTTING

LIGHT

MIRROR

FIG. 13.—Cutting bench.

economic use of material. The cutline indicates the number of shapes required of each colour. If it is not easy to see how these shapes can be cut from the sheet with economy, the shapes may be traced off on to scrap paper. The templates, cut out in paper, may be moved about on the glass until a suitable formation is discovered which will cause a minimum of waste. When the positions are ascertained, the glass sheet should be placed conveniently on the cutting bench with the traced cutline beneath.

When cutting straight lines or lines curving slightly, very little difficulty is experienced in obtaining good results, because the cuts are in keeping with the natural character of the glass; they are the sort of lines that might occur through accidental breakage.

FIG. 14.—Glass shapes easily cut.

Fig. 14 shows some glass shapes in keeping with the natural qualities of the material. To cut shapes such as these, the first incision should be made to follow one of the lines of the cutline and continue in order to separate the piece required from the sheet.

Fig. 15 illustrates how, in cutting the shape XPQY from the irregular glass sheet, the workman would make use of the straight edge for his line PQ and his first incision would be from A to B. This cut would give him the side XY required

30

for his shape, and at the same time it would separate his piece in bulk from the main sheet. If the unwanted part of the glass is too small to be of any future use, two or three smart taps with

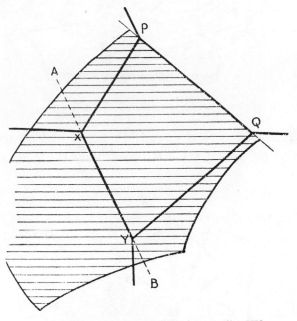

FIG. 15.—Direct cut AB, along cutline XY.
Lines XP and YQ are cut afterwards.

the heel of the cutter along, and on the opposite side to, the incision will cause the unwanted portion to break away cleanly. Fig. 16 shows how the glass should be held when tapping along the incision. The shape that is to be retained should be held lightly in one hand over a rubbish box, into which the unwanted pieces may be allowed to fall.

31

If the pieces on each side of a cut are wanted, being of useful size, the glass should be tapped

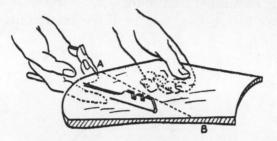

FIG. 16.—Tapping the cut AB in Fig. 15.

over a bench so that neither piece will be splintered by a long fall. Alternatively the glass may

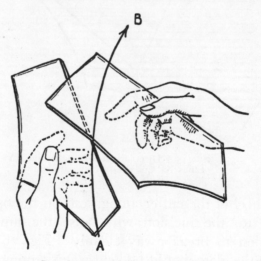

FIG. 17.—Scraping glass, right hand moving from A to B.

be held each side of the cut, and the back of the glass opposite the cut tapped smartly on the corner of a bench. Only more or less straight cuts can be made in this manner. When a cut has been made the edge of the piece of glass to be retained should be scraped. To scrape the edge, a piece of glass is held in each hand and the edges scraped together with a sliding motion, upwards with one hand and downwards with the other (Fig. 17). All the edges should be dealt with in this way, thus reducing the possibility of a nasty cut during the frequent handling at future

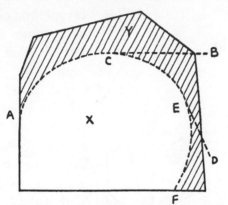

FIG. 18.—Cutting shape X, first cut AB, second cut CD, third cut, EF.

stages. Incidentally, never be tempted to catch a falling piece of glass, as a serious accident may be caused in this way.

Although the designs for stained glass work should be built up from simple glass shapes, it sometimes occurs that a strained and unnatural shape cannot be avoided. The cutting of such shapes, for instance those including concave curves, often results in a waste of glass and time.

If it is borne in mind that glass always tends to break at the weakest part, special precautions may be taken to avoid breaking awkward shapes when cutting. Should the design include lead lines which resemble a slice of bread from which a bite has been taken it will be obvious how cutting difficulties arise. The glass shape representing the bitten portion can be cut out in a straightforward manner (Fig. 18), but the shape representing the remainder of the slice introduces cutting complications. The best method of cutting out shapes of this sort is first to cut round the concave line and then to make a series of concentric incisions on the waste portion (Fig. 19). Each cut should be taken up to the edge of the glass at intervals of about an eighth of an inch for normal work, though for large work more space may be allowed between the parallel incisions. The main consideration is thoroughly to weaken the waste portion.

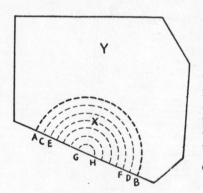

FIG. 19.—Cutting shape Y, first cut AB, second cut CD. Tap from A and B towards centre.

When all the incisions have been made the cuts may be tapped, beginning at both edges of the glass and working towards the centre. Before all the cuts have been tapped the waste glass

34

should fall away, but if it continues to hold after considerable tapping the unwanted portion may

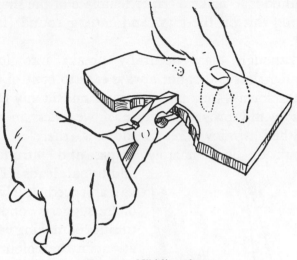

FIG. 20.—Nibbling glass.

be nibbled away with the glaziers' pliers (Fig. 20).

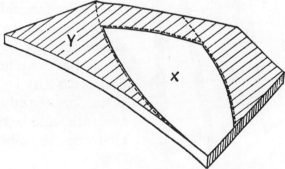

FIG. 21.—Cutting shape X from dark glass.
Make template in tracing paper and cut round.

Now a few general points with regard to cutting.

35

Dark glass requires to be cut on some sort of bench with illumination from beneath. Another method is to make a paper template of the shape, laying this on the glass and cutting round (Fig. 21).

Although glass naturally breaks into long slender shapes it is not always easy to control the cut to form a long narrow point, and in any case this would prove a feature of weakness in the finished window. It is stronger, therefore, to break up long narrow shapes and introduce additional leads (Fig. 22), a procedure which often suggests opportunities of making variations in the colour of the glass components.

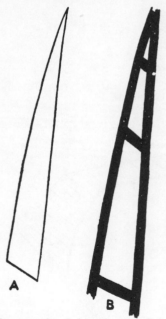

When cutting a glass shape the most difficult edge should be attempted first, as this allows for any adjustment that may be required should the curve be slightly inaccurate and require recutting or nibbling (Fig. 23).

FIG. 22.—Leads introduced in B for greater strength and change of glass.

Make it a rule to avoid shapes with sharp curves cut out of them (the bitten slice). Similar shapes, with definite angles cut from them

(**Fig.** 24) are impossible to cut with any degree of success or safety. All awkward features of the

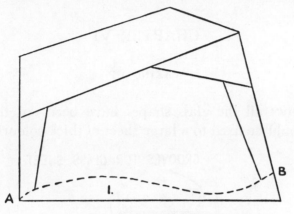

FIG. 23.—Cut AB first to allow for adjustment.

design should be reduced to simple shapes by the introduction of additional leads.

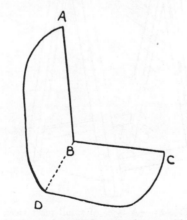

FIG. 24.—Angles such as ABC cannot be cut with safety.
Introduce lead at BD.

37

CHAPTER VI

WAXING UP

WHEN all the glass shapes have been cut they
should be fixed to a large sheet of thick colourless

GROOVES FOR GLASS SHEET

FIG. 25.—A type of small glass easel.

glass so that the pieces may be seen together in
their proper relationship.   By mounting the

pieces in this way a clear idea of the general colour scheme of the window may be obtained.

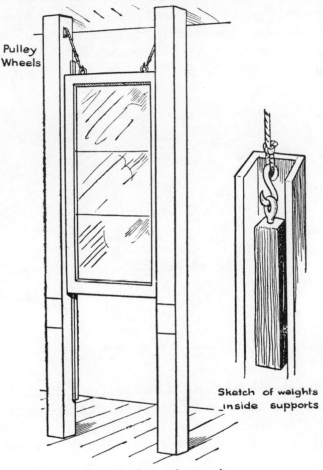

FIG. 26.—Large glass easel.

Plate glass is the most satisfactory for mounting purposes though not absolutely necessary. Small unframed sheets of glass, three or four feet in length, may be used by sliding them into a glass easel with grooved sides (Fig. 25). For larger work plate glass is required. This should be framed in stout wood and hung from iron hooks at the top. It is desirable that the height of the plate-glass panel should be variable and, in view of the weight of the panel, a pair of strong

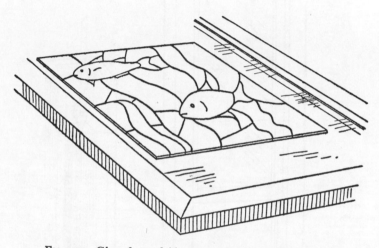

FIG. 27.—Glass frame laid on cartoon for waxing up.

supports are needed. These supports should be hollow to allow the movement of counter-balance weights which support the plate glass panel in any position, similar to a sash window (Fig. 26). The supports should be as high as possible to permit windows being fixed on the plate glass at the heights above the eye level, as where windows are being made for positions above eye level it is important that the worker should see his work in the same relative position whilst he is engaged upon it at this stage.

For the process of waxing up the cartoon is laid on a flat bench and the glass panel placed on top (Fig. 27). Using the cutline for a guide the pieces of cut glass are laid on the panel in their

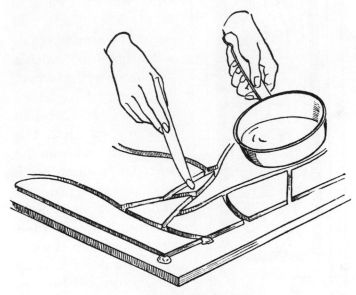

FIG. 28.—Waxing up.

correct positions, each piece being separated from the next by a distance representing the core of the lead. When all the parts are correctly placed a drop of molten beeswax is applied to every corner of each separate piece of glass. This process must be carried out both accurately and speedily. It must be done accurately, for the beeswax must fall on the corner of the glass and nowhere else. If only a very small portion of wax comes in contact with the surface of the glass, the greasy state will prevent pigment from settling during the painting process. It must be done speedily because the liquid wax soon hardens in the atmosphere and requires warming again.

The beeswax, which is purchased in the form of cakes, may be warmed up in an old saucepan over the gas jet. For taking the wax from the saucepan a suitable tool is a narrow-pointed splinter of glass or piece of metal. Sufficient molten wax may be picked up on the point to drop quickly on to the required position (Fig. 28). Plasticine may be used instead of wax for fixing the glass and in some ways it is preferable, for it allows frequent removal and replacement of the glass shapes without the need to take the panel down from the vertical position.

FIG. 29.—The glass waxed up for inspection of colour scheme and ready for painting. The shapes and colour pattern of the glass should give some idea of the subject of the window.

When the glass shapes are waxed up the window

is mounted up vertically. Although the combinations of coloured glass can be examined a thorough appreciation is impossible because the colour scheme is affected by the lines of bright light where the opaque lead should be. To remedy this, black lines, representing the leads, are painted on the back of the plate glass panel. In addition any uncovered glass bordering the window should be blacked out with paint (lamp black, vegetable black or poster paint) so that a true appearance of the window is presented for examination. Fig. 29 shows a window waxed up. The smooth sides of the glass shapes now face the workman, for these represent the inside of the window, the side on which the paint will be applied.

CHAPTER VII

LEADING UP, SOLDERING AND CEMENTING

ALTHOUGH these are the final processes of the craft, as a reference to Chapter II will show, they are dealt with here in order that they may be in the most useful sequence for anyone wishing to

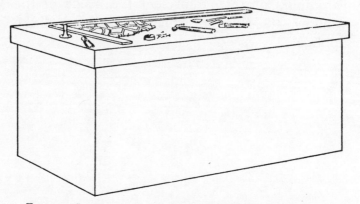

FIG. 30.—Leading up bench. A firm bench with gas jet fitted for soldering connections.

make a window which does not include any painting or staining. Elementary work in the craft should be of this sort, providing exercise in colour pattern and the techniques of glass cutting, leading up, etc.

It is worth while, if possible, to have a separate

room for leading up, because the process is rather dirty and untidy, though the case is usually met by having part of the single room set aside for the purpose.

These are the requirements for the process:

1. **Bench.** (Fig. 30). This should have a flat top of wood and have a gas jet connection at one end.

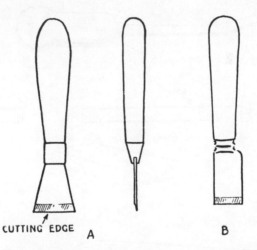

CUTTING EDGE   A   B

FIG. 31.—A, Cutting Knife. B, Improvised household knife.

2. **Lead Cutting Knife.** (Fig. 31). This may be improvised from an old paint scraper, palette- or table-knife. The blade is sharpened so that the edge is at right angles to the handle. When cutting a lead the knife is held vertically and pressure is applied evenly to make a clean cut. Careless cutting wastes material and increases the difficulties of fitting the glass into the leads.

3. **A Lathekin.** (Fig. 32). This is a bent piece of metal, rounded and smooth at one end. It is used to open the leads before fitting the glass. A six inch nail, ground at the point and fitted with a handle, makes a serviceable improvised lathekin. Bone and wood may also be used.

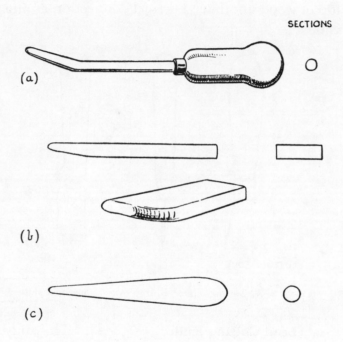

SECTIONS

(a)

(b)

(c)

Fig. 32.—Lathekins (a) metal; (b) wood; (c) bone.

4. **Hammer and Stopping Knife.** (Fig. 33). This is usually constructed by fitting a disc of lead on the handle of a stopping knife or lathekin; it is often convenient to have two tools in the hand

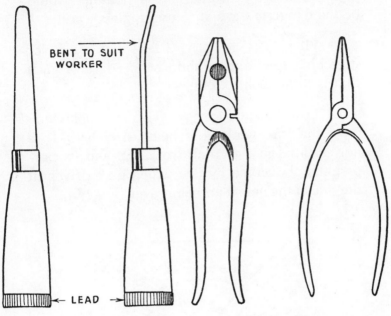

FIG. 33.—Hammer and stopping knife.

FIG. 34.—Pliers.

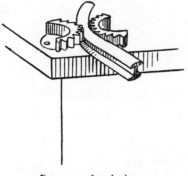

FIG. 35.—Lead vice.

FIG. 36.—Improvised lead-vice of two bent nails.

at once, and the ordinary iron hammer would be too dangerous a tool to use in glass work.

5. **Pliers.** (Fig. 34). Pliers are used for stretching lead and nibbling the edges of glass that is troublesome to fit.

6. **Lead-Vice.** (Fig. 35). This is a tool which grips the lead while it is being stretched. It is not essential in the small workshop and its purpose may be served by two strong nails driven in the side of the bench and bent over (Fig. 36).

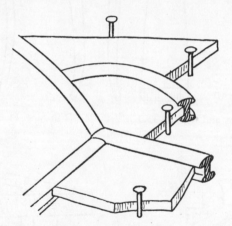

FIG. 37.—Small nails holding glass in position.

7. **Nails.** Small nails are used to hold the glass in position before it is surrounded by lead (Fig. 37).

8. **Laths or Battens.** These are nailed to the bench and used to hold the window together during the work of leading up (Fig. 38).

48

The Process of Leading Up. The cutline is laid on the bench and the wooden laths are firmly nailed across at one corner forming a right angle (Fig. 38). Although the cutline will show a narrow border representing the core of the framing lead, a slight extra space must be allowed outside this when nailing the laths down on the cutline (See AB, Fig. 39).

The leads used for the frame of the window should be wider than those used for inside work. For most reasonably-sized windows ½" calm is used for the outside edges and ⅜" calm for the inside.

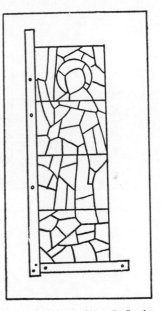

FIG. 38.—Plan of bench. Laths nailed to bench for leading up. Showing cartoon of sectional window.

Before commencing work all tools should be ready at hand and the glass shapes placed near and in rotation. If the shapes are waxed up on a frame they may be removed one at a time and leaded up. Before using the lead it is stretched to strengthen, toughen and straighten it. One end may be placed in the lead-vice and the other held by pliers and pulled strongly (Fig. 40). After the lead has stretched a little it usually breaks off at the vice or the pliers. Very long

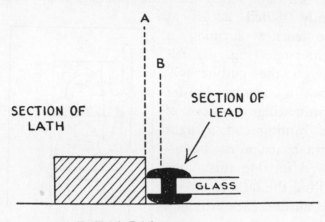

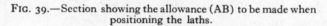

FIG. 39.—Section showing the allowance (AB) to be made when positioning the laths.

FIG. 40.—Pulling lead.

pieces of calm may be stretched by two people pulling on it, each holding an end with pliers. Short lengths may be held down on the ground with the foot and pulled upwards (Fig. 41).

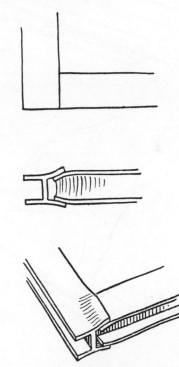

FIG. 41.—Holding lead by foot for stretching.

FIG. 42.—The right-angled joint lapped.

Two lengths of wide calm should be cut off and placed against the laths to form two edges of the window. These leads should be an inch or so longer than the actual size of the window and should be lapped together for a corner joint (Fig. 42). The first piece of glass should now be fitted

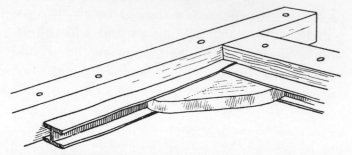

FIG. 43.—The first piece of glass fitted to the right angle.

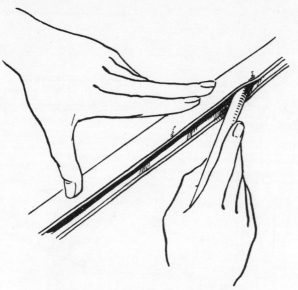

FIG. 44.—Widening leads with lathekin.

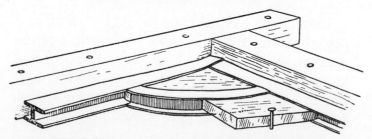

FIG. 45.—The lead and the second piece of glass fitted.

up tightly into the right angle formed by the calms (Fig. 43). This should now be hedged in with narrower calm. The method is to chop off a piece of lead a little longer than required. One end should be fitted to the glass and cut to the correct angle to form a joint with the outside calm. (Note that joints other than at the four corners need not be lapped, butt joints will suffice.) When one end of the calm has been fitted it should be bent round the glass shape and the other end marked off to fit with a knife scratch, and cut to length. The cutting tends to press the lips of the calm together and the lead should be opened out with the lathekin (Fig. 44). A second piece of glass may now be fitted and held in position for leading by a nail or two lightly tapped in the bench *vertically* (Fig. 45). Where several nails are used to hold a piece of glass they should carefully follow the cutline and act as a check to the leading up in general (Fig. 46).

Finally, when all the glass shapes are leaded, another two pieces of wide calm are fitted along the open edges and lapped at the corners. Any extra length of calm at the corners is cut off to size and laths are nailed along the other two sides (Fig. 47). Finally, the corners of the window should be checked for right angles, with a square or the corner of a box, and the window is now ready for soldering.

Doubling. This is a process in which two

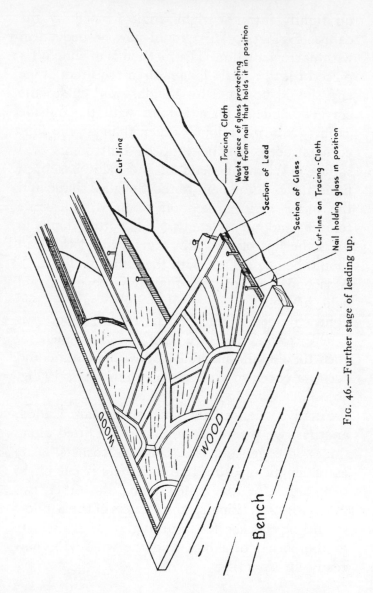

Cut-line

Tracing Cloth

Waste piece of glass protecting
lead from nail that holds it in position

Section of Lead

Section of Glass

Cut-line on Tracing-Cloth

Nail holding glass in position

WOOD

WOOD

Bench

Fig. 46.—Further stage of leading up.

54

thicknesses of glass are leaded up together to obtain different varieties of colour effects. Sometimes the design for the window calls for such special colouring of one or two shapes that only doubling, in conjunction with etching (See Chapter IX) and silver staining (See Chapter X),

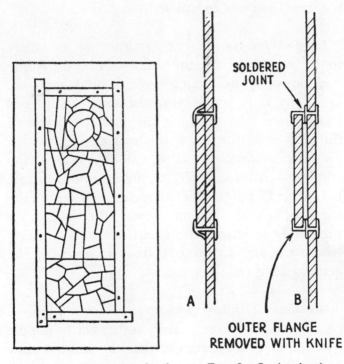

SOLDERED
JOINT

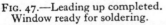

A   B

OUTER FLANGE
REMOVED WITH KNIFE

FIG. 47.—Leading up completed. Window ready for soldering.

FIG. 48.—Section showing methods of doubling.

can produce the desired results. Fig. 48 shows two methods of doubling; 'A' shows the use of leads with double depth cores, while 'B' shows the use of ordinary size calm with the outside flange removed. In the first method the doubled glass is leaded up with the rest of the window, but in the second method the doubled shape may be soldered on later. This procedure (B) is very helpful should it be required to alter the colour effect of some particular glass shape after the window has been completed.

Large Windows. Large windows are too heavy to be supported by the leads alone and some methods of strengthening have to be introduced. One way is to use steel-cored calm (i.e. leads having steel wire running through the centre of the lead core) for a few of the lead lines which play an important part in the structure of the window. Alternatively, or in addition, saddle bars (See Chapter XII) may be used across the window, either cutting across the design or preferably in conjunction with sectional leading where the horizontal bar lines fit in with the general design of the window.

Sectional Window Leading. Large windows can be made stronger, safer, and easier to handle by arranging the design so that the window may be made in separate sections which fit into each other. The size of the sections will vary according to the size of the window, but as most panels tend to be tall and narrow the sections will usually be horizontal. With very large windows both horizontal and vertical sections are used and these are fitted into a network of iron bars fitted into the window frame.

Here we will confine ourselves to the smaller panel, divided into horizontal sections only, for the methods can be applied equally well to the vertical sectioning.

The top section is fitted with a side lead of normal-depth core along the horizontal edge forming the outside of the window. The lower horizontal edge is fitted with a wide lead of double-depth core. All the sections are similarly made, single-depth core lead along the top and

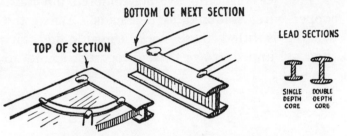

FIG. 49.—Joint between window sections.

double-depth core lead along the bottom, except the last section which has single-depth at both top and bottom.

All the side leads are single depth, matching the horizontal ones in width. Thus at every horizontal bar in the window a single-depth core lead fits into a double one (Fig. 49) and the flanges of the deeper lead overlap the shallower one. To make a strong joint the outer flanges of the inside lead are pressed inwards, one over the other, with the lathekin (Fig. 50). To bend these flanges the panel is laid flat on the bench and the upper flange bent downwards, the panel is then turned over and the other one pressed tightly down.

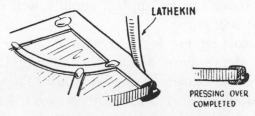

FIG. 50.—Pressing down a flange.

These section joints are not soldered but have copper wires soldered to the leads. When the window is fitted these wires coincide in pairs (Fig. 51) and they are twisted together round an

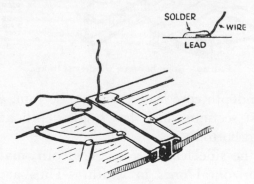

FIG. 51.—Two soldered sections showing method of fitting together and wires for fixing to window bar.

iron window or saddle bar (Figs. 79 and 80) holding the sections firmly in place. The wires and iron bar are largely concealed by the wide horizontal lead line.

Soldering. Before commencing this process the window should be carefully examined to see that the corners are right angles and that the outside leads are straight. The following tools and materials are required:

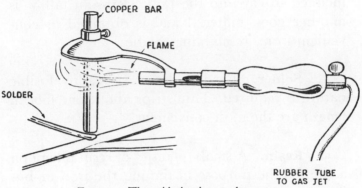

FIG. 52.—The soldering iron and process.

1. **Soldering Iron.** (Fig. 52). The type of iron used for stained glass work consists of a cylindrical copper bar on which a gas flame plays continually. The gas is led through the handle of the tool and the flame heats a copper face which comes into contact with the solder. The degree of heat can be regulated both by an attachment on the burner and by the gas tap on the bench. Care must be taken not to get the iron too hot or some of the window lead may melt whilst a joint is being soldered. The copper face must be kept flat and clean, with the use of a file, to ensure clean and sound work.

2. **File.** Used to keep the soldering iron in good working condition.

3. **Flux.** Flux is necessary to clean the surface of the lead and cause the solder to run. Killed spirits are often used, and though they are easy to handle care must be taken thoroughly to clean the window afterwards as the acid is inclined to eat into the lead. Russian tallow is another good material and is obtained in convenient forms resembling candles.

4. **Solder.** Lead solder of a readily fusible nature is required. Thin strips about one foot in length are the most convenient.

5. **Resin.** A small quantity of resin is kept on a tile for the purpose of tinning the iron or bit. The iron is tinned ready for use by heating until a green flame is seen, filing the end, plunging into the resin and picking up a piece of solder from the tile.

6. **Rags.** These are useful for cleaning all joints before applying flux.

7. **Brush.** A wire or stiff-bristled scrubbing brush may also be used for cleaning joints before soldering. This is only necessary when the window has been left for some time and the lead has become tarnished.

The Process of Soldering. In the production of a good window each stage depends for success upon the accuracy of the previous stage. This is particularly true in the case of soldering, which depends upon the accuracy of the joints in the leading up operation. The closer the joints have been fitted the better the soldered joint will be. Small spaces in joints can be filled with solder, but it is unreasonable to expect the solder to fill large gaps in place of lead.

The joints on the upper side of the window are first cleaned by rubbing briskly with rags or brush; tarnish, grease or dirt of any kind will prevent the solder running. Next the joints are treated liberally with flux, either tallow or spirits. The stick of solder is then held in one hand and the soldering iron in the other. The end of the stick of solder is placed on the joint and the tip of the iron on that, causing a blob of solder to form on the joint. A short movement of the iron each way along the leads to be joined will make a strong smooth finish. If the solder will not run the cause is usually dirt either on the joint, the solder, the iron or the flux.

When all the joints on the upper side of the window have been soldered all the surplus flux should be wiped off with a rag. The surrounding laths may now be removed from the bench and the window turned over with great care. The joints on the second side are now soldered.

NOTE. If the final mounting of the window requires saddle bars (see Chapter XII), copper wires must be soldered on to the horizontal lead lines at this stage. The wires should be four or five inches in length, soldered in the middle to a horizontal lead bar preferably at a point where a vertical lead line joins, so that the construction is concealed as far as possible (Fig. 53). In sectional window work the end of the wire is soldered to the lead and care should be taken to

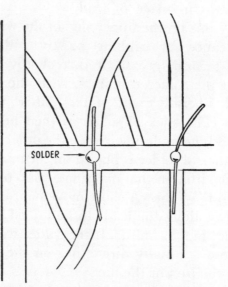

SOLDER

FIG. 53.—Showing supporting wires opposite vertical leads.

see that pairs of wires correspond where the sections fit together (Fig. 79).

Cementing. This is the final stage in the construction of the window and the full quality of the previous work cannot be appreciated until this is completed.

Cement for windows is made by mixing equal quantities of whiting and plaster of Paris together with turpentine and boiled linseed oil to make a thick paste. Lamp black is added to darken the colour of the mixture, while red lead is added if the window is to be exposed to the elements. The cement may be stored in a large airtight tin.

The window to be cemented is laid flat on the bench and the cement is dabbed on to the window with the aid of a stick. A stiff-bristled scrubbing brush is then used to force the cement between the glass and the leads (Fig. 54). To do this the brush

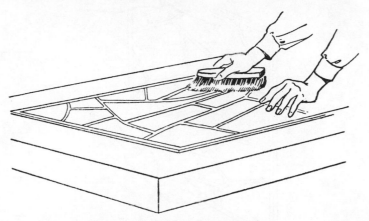

FIG. 54.—Cementing a leaded panel.

must be rubbed vigorously in every direction and each piece of glass must be treated individually. The wooden stick with which the window is daubed with cement may be used to rub along the leads and press them down smoothly after cementing.

The window should now be turned over and the process repeated. If the first side has been well done some of the mixture will be seen oozing through to the other side when the window is turned.

The process is completed by putting whiting on the panel and well scrubbing until the glass is clean and the leads are bright and shining. The window should now be placed carefully on one side to allow the cement to harden and set.

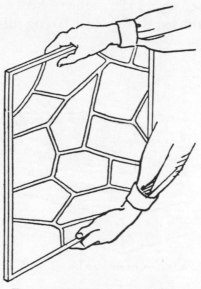

FIG. 55.—Handling a leaded panel.

NOTE. When handling panels of leaded glass they should be moved in such a way that there is no tendency for the panel to bend. The safest method is to hold the window edgeways to the floor, taking the weight on the lower hand and merely holding the panel in position with the upper hand (Fig. 55). To attempt to take the weight with the upper hand may result in the leads being strained apart, especially in the case of heavy windows. When laying panels flat on

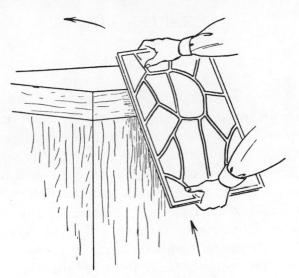

FIG. 56.—Laying a leaded panel flat.

the bench use the edge of the bench to support the weight while sliding the window across from the vertical carrying position (Fig. 56).

CHAPTER VIII

PAINTING ON GLASS

THE problems that face the painter of stained glass are quite different from those which occur in other pictorial work. The paint or pigment for glass work is an oxide in powder form which is mixed with water, painted on, and then fired into the glass so that it fuses and becomes part of the basic material. The palette of the glass worker is restricted to a very limited range of opaque colours, composed mainly of oxides of iron. The colours range from reddish brown to black and when applied strongly they completely prevent light passing through the glass. In all the work the paint must be applied confidently to obtain intense opacity; retouched and niggled painting will usually 'fry' (See Chapter XI) during firing. In addition to intense opaque painting there are various methods of shading which greatly influence the general colours and quality of the window.

The primary consideration in the application of the pigment should be that the light is to fall from behind, through the glass and into the interior. When the light in the interior is stronger than the outside the effects of colouring and painting are concealed. This feature of limitation should be used to evolve a technique suited to the medium, while the technique must be adapted to the special purpose for which the window is intended. The development of technique should be natural and no attempt should be made to force a style by rigidly copying the methods of others. Interesting decorative treatments may be examined and their interest analysed for personal use, but wholesale imitation will deny the pleasure of experiment and produce lifeless work lacking originality.

When the pigment is added to the glass it sticks comparatively securely (due to a proportion of gum arabic added to the oxide mixture). The nature of the adhering pigment offers great scope in decorative treatment by way of scratching, stippling, etc. Such treatment is admirably suited to the character of work through which light passes and is the means of obtaining some most interesting qualities in the glass which must not be overlooked when tracing from the cartoon. It might be imagined that careful tracing from the cartoon would be conducive to accuracy but the fact is that true glass technique cannot be represented on paper. Even where the degree of representation is very close, it can only be obtained by a tremendous amount of unnecessary work. The cartoon should, therefore, be only a reference to the general idea of the subject and the glass designer, after a few preliminary brush strokes traced from his cartoon, soon becomes absorbed in the painting of the glass itself.

As will be remembered from Chapter VI we have reached the stage when the window is waxed up with the flat surface of glass shapes facing the workman ready for painting (Fig. 29).

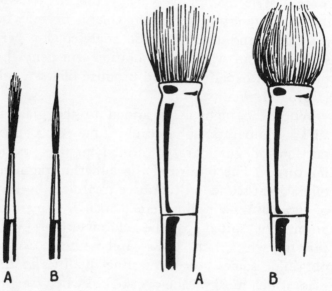

FIG. 57.—The Rigger. A, dry. B, wet.

FIG. 58.—The mop or wash brush. A, dry. B, wet.

Now, before dealing with the next process in detail, we will enumerate the equipment which the glass painter requires. The equipment is usually a very personal matter and most of the implements can be improvised from scrap pieces of wood, bone, and metal, and from brushes of various kinds. The usual set of brushes, tools and material required are :

1. **Liner or Rigger.** (Fig. 57). This is a long-haired brush, soft and flexible, with a fine, slender point. Any tracing and delicate line work is usually done with the liner, and the painter should possess a selection of various sizes.

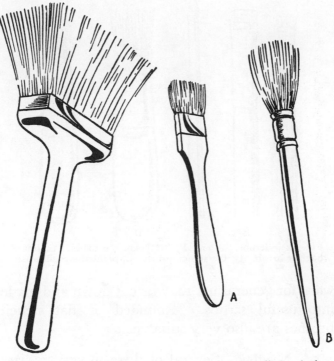

FIG. 59.—The Badger.   FIG. 60.—A, small flat badger. B, round badger.

2. **Mop or Wash Brush.** (Fig. 58). A soft-haired brush capable of holding a considerable amount of pigment for applying washes.

69

3. **Badgers.** (Figs. 59 and 60). Thick long-badger haired brushes for 'matting'.

4. **Hoghair Brushes or Scrubs.** (Fig. 61.) A selection of stiff short-haired brushes for brushing off pigment before it has been fired. Discarded brushes of various types and sizes that are too

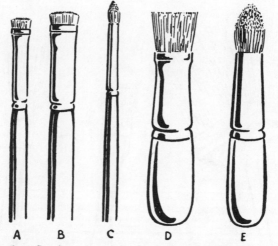

A   B   C   D   E

FIG. 61.—Scrubs. A and B, flat hoghair brushes. C, round hoghair brush. D, flat stencil brush. E, pointed stencil brush.

worn for general use may be cut down and made into useful scrubs. Rounded or flat stencil brushes are also very suitable.

5. **Needles.** Several of these in various sizes are necessary to provide a variety in technique. The ends of brush handles may be sharpened to suitable points or pointed pieces of wood, bone or metal may be used. Knitting needles may be employed and very useful tools can be impro-

vised by embedding gramophone needles in the ends of sticks.

6. **The Pigment.** Reliable varieties may be purchased quite cheaply and the personal preparation of pigment is rarely worth while. The pigment is supplied as a powder in tins or packets.

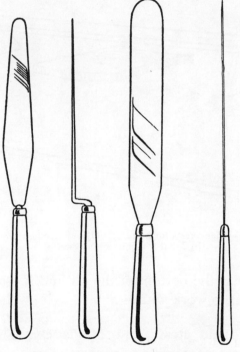

FIG. 62.—Two styles of palette knives.

7. **The Palette.** Thick plate glass is the most suitable. The glass should not be too small as the pigment spreads out when working.

8. **The Palette Knife.** (Fig. 62). A flexible palette knife is required for grinding the pigment.

71

9. **Gum.** A few drops of gum arabic mixed with the pigment prevent it being rubbed off the glass too easily.

10. **Water Jar.** The same jar should be used continually when working with one paint as the pigment which washes from the brushes forms a

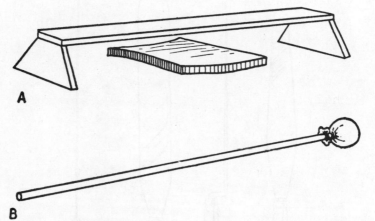

A

B

FIG. 63.—Hand rests for painting. (a) For tracing from cartoon. (b) Maul for painting at easel.

residue at the bottom of the jar and is often very pleasant to work with.

11. **Hand Rests and Maulstick.** (Fig. 63). These greatly assist the process of painting. The rests are made of wood and, as can be seen from the sketch, are easily constructed.

Preparation of Pigment for Painting. Some powdered pigment should be shaken out on to a clean sheet of glass—the palette. The pigment

72

should be used liberally to avoid running short of paint in the middle of an interesting piece of work. Add water and thoroughly mix with the palette knife to a creamy consistency. Add a few drops of gum arabic and grind well until the gum is evenly distributed, all gritty particles of the pigment have disappeared and the paint is smooth and satin-like in quality. The best results can only be obtained by sound mixing. Too much gum in the mixture may cause 'frying'.

The Application and Treatment of the Paint. The paint should be applied fluently and smoothly. Thick and retouched work will result in 'frying'.

1. **Line Work.** The main lines of the design are first lightly painted on. They may be traced directly from the cartoon or sketched freely on the glass according to the method and ability of the painter. In the case of tracing, the waxed up window would be over the cartoon and in a horizontal position on the bench. Here the use of hand rests will permit greater control of brushwork and enable easier manipulation when tracing curves. As soon as the tracing can be dispensed with, the window should be mounted in a vertical position for the remainder of the painting. For working with the window in this upright position a maulstick (Fig. 64) will be necessary to steady the hand holding the brush. It should be remembered that paint will not run

uphill, so, as far as possible, the shaft of the brush
should be kept above the point of the hairs.

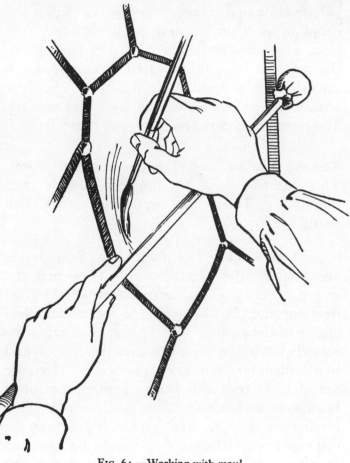

FIG. 64.—Working with maul.

2. **Stippling and Matting.** The paint is
brushed on to the glass with the wash brush and
while it is still wet it is stippled or matted.

In stippling the badger brush is dabbed on the pigment, the brush being held at right angles to the glass in a manner similar to stencilling technique. This treatment is generally used as a preliminary stage to matting, though it is sometimes left to form a decorative feature in itself.

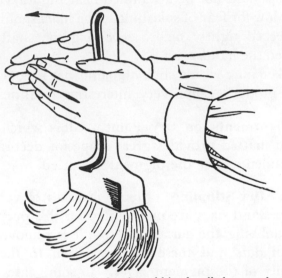

FIG. 65.—Drying the badger by rubbing handle between hands.

When matting is to follow, the stippling must be done quickly before all the moisture evaporates. The matting process consists of drawing the badger across the pigmented glass in different directions until a fine, even distribution is obtained.

For good results the badger must be clean and dry and the pigment well ground. If the paint is worked too long it may form into undesirable

75

ridges. To clean the badger it should be rinsed in water, when the pigment will quickly leave the hairs. It must now be dried so that the hairs stand out separately and are soft and sensitive. To dry the brush hold the handle between the palms of the hands and rub vigorously (Fig. 65). This should not be attempted near the waxed up window for fear of splashing. The hairs should be squeezed tightly before revolving the shaft between the hands.

Sketching with a stick on paint that is not quite dry produces some very interesting qualities.

Treatments on Dry Paint. Glass which has been matted provides great scope for decorative treatments after the pigment has dried.

1. **Dry Stippling.** Stencil brushes of various shapes and sizes are most suited for this purpose. By dabbing the surface the paint is removed in small dots and these give variation to the intensity of the pigment layer. In some cases this method is employed to model form and gives the impression of solidity to objects by creating an illusion of light and shade. But its greatest value is to improve the quality of the glass.

2. **Trimming.** Lines may be trimmed and corrected before firing where necessary. Tools for this may be improvised from the sharpened ends of brushes.

3. **Stick Lights.** As the name suggests,

sharpened sticks are used to remove matted painting and add sparkle to the glass in the form of small dots, diamonds, stars, etc. This method may also be used for other decorative treatments such as pattern, and by experiment the painter will find this technique offers a wide field of effects.

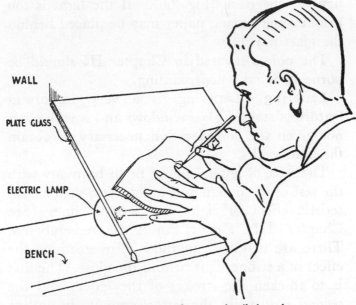

WALL

PLATE GLASS

ELECTRIC LAMP

BENCH

FIG. 66.—Arrangement for very detailed work.

4. **Brushing.** This is similar to dry stippling, but dry hair brushes of the oil painter's type are used instead of stencil brushes and the paint is brushed off the glass.

Though much of the painting may be done when the window is waxed up and in a vertical position, some of the special pigment treatments are facilitated by removing the shapes and dealing with them separately, waxing up again afterwards to inspect the effect as a whole. A useful arrangement when dealing with the separate shapes is to rest the shape for stippling against a piece of white glass at 45° having an electric light at the back (Fig. 66). If the light is too bright some tracing paper may be placed behind the glass panel.

The points stressed in Chapter III should be borne in mind when painting.

Lettering. Lettering is a very important feature of stained glass windows and is very often not given the consideration necessary to obtain the best results.

The style of letters should be in harmony with the rest of the design and in addition the characteristic effect of light on painted lines (See Chapter III, Fig. 1) must be remembered. There are two main methods of overcoming the effect of a strong light behind the glass. The first is to thicken the strokes of the letters and the second is to paint the letters strongly in outline so that the colour of the glass is seen in the actual strokes of each letter. Still further to assist the legibility of the letters a thin matt background of paint will partly subdue the brilliance and sparkle of the light which unsubdued confuses the eyes.

CHAPTER IX

ETCHING

THIS process utilizes flashed glass (See Chapter I) and consists of removing part of the thin layer of flashing with acid, revealing the colour of the base glass beneath (Fig. 67). In this way two

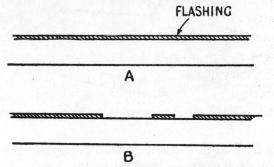

FIG. 67—(a) Section of flashed glass (enlarged).
(b) Section of glass that has been etched.

colours may be used in the design without the introduction of an unwanted lead line. After having been etched the glass may be painted and /or silver stained as desired.

The Process. The acid employed is hydroflouric, which, when undiluted, is an extremely potent liquid. Because of its rapid action on glass it should be kept in a well-corked guttapercha receptacle which will not allow the unpleasant fumes to escape. Should the fingers come into contact with the acid when handling they should be washed immediately. The effect on the skin is not immediately apparent but the acid if not washed away will penetrate the pores and cause pain later on. The instructor in stained glass work should practise etching away from his students and finally show them with confidence

FIG. 68.—Dabbing acid when only a small area of glass is to be removed.

the safest and most satisfactory method he has found of handling the acid. In any case it is unwise to allow young students to use undiluted acid by themselves.

The glass shape to be treated with acid should be placed on a bench over the cartoon and the parts of the glass not to be treated are coated with wax. This may be applied to the glass in a molten state with a brush and trimmed, if necessary, when cold with a knife. Another method is to pour warm wax on to warm glass and further heat the glass over a gas jet so that the wax spreads in an even coat over the surface.

As before the parts to be treated with acid may be scraped clean to match the cartoon. Whenever possible the area to be etched should be surrounded with wax to hold the acid in position. A few drops of concentrated acid should be dropped on to the glass and dabbed into all the angles that have to be treated. A small piece of cloth may be screwed into a ball and tied to the end of a stick for use as a dabber (Fig. 68).

Fig. 69.—Using a splinter to control glass in acid bath.

Sometimes very large areas of glass have to be etched, leaving only small portions of flashing untouched. For this the glass should be covered with wax on both sides and edges, the parts to be etched scraped clear, and the whole piece submerged in a gutta-percha bath of diluted acid. To control the glass in the acid bath a piece of wooden stick or a splinter of glass should be used (Fig. 69) which can be destroyed afterwards. The splinter when not in use should be left in the acid bath out of danger.

To remove the glass from the bath the stick

should be used to lever up one corner clear of the acid, then take hold of this corner with the thumb and finger (Fig. 70). The glass should be held downwards over the acid bath for a moment or so to allow surplus acid to drip off. Glass and fingers should then be immersed in a bucket of water kept at hand. The water in this bucket should be changed frequently, otherwise it will become virtually a dilute solution of acid and will not be effective for rinsing the hands.

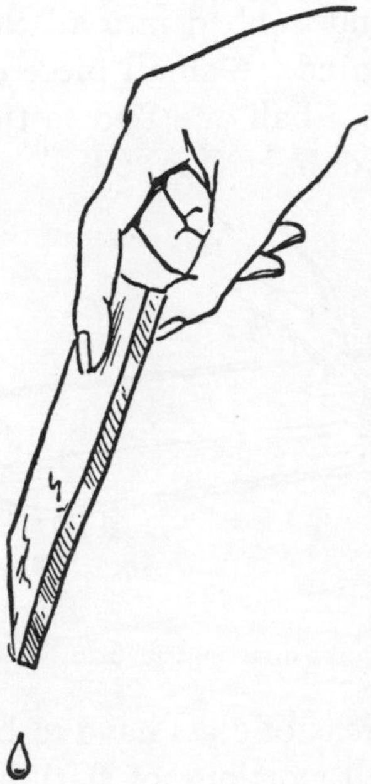

After etching, the wax may be removed from the glass by gently heating in the gas flame.

The length of time that the glass requires under the action of acid depends upon the thickness of the

FIG. 70.—Removing glass from acid bath.

glass to be removed and the strength of the acid. The exact time can easily be discovered by experience, using a small piece of the same glass as a test piece, removing from the acid periodically to examine the condition, and noting just how long is necessary for the desired effect. If the acid is at full strength the etching process may last only a few minutes. Care must be taken to avoid over-action of the acid which, apart from weakening the glass, gives the glass a cloudy appearance.

As mentioned in Chapter I, the most common type of flashed glass is red or ruby on white. By etching we may produce the effect of a white design on a red background or vice versa, according to the amount and arrangement of flashing removed. In addition a skilful craftsman can control the acid in such a way that the etching is graduated, giving the appearance of the flash colour merging into the colour of the base glass. If this is done with such combinations as a red flash on blue glass there will be a merging of the blue through purple to red.

Another method of producing some interesting colour experiments is by combining etching with 'doubling' (See Chapter VII). For instance, by doubling two pieces of flashed glass, one of green glass flashed with blue and the other of white glass flashed with red, and by carefully graduating the etching of each, a great variety of colours can be effected.

Finally, silver stain may be added (See Chapter X) to the variously etched glass, plain or flashed, single thickness or double, resulting in further colour combinations including the greens and oranges.

It is important to realize that over-interest in these processes may easily lead to the loss of the true character of stained glass, in which the lead lines are an integral part of the enrichment of the window as a whole.

CHAPTER X

THIS stain may be mixed from ingredients, but it is more satisfactory to purchase it in a prepared state. It is in the form of powder and should be mixed with water and ground carefully with a palette knife for fifteen or twenty minutes until it is a deep mustard colour. A little gum may be added to make it easier to handle.

The silver stain is applied to the back of the glass, i.e., the outside of the window, and is fired after the painting has been fired, as it is generally heated to a lower temperature. On drawing from the kiln an opaque scum will be found on the glass where stain has been applied. The scum is easily removed by wiping with a rag and the colour of the staining may be considered for suitability. The depth of colour produced will depend upon the concentration of the stain and the firing. If the colour is too light a second coat may be fired on. As with etching it is a good plan to try the stain on a scrap piece of the same glass and find out the best firing temperature by experiment.

The usual method of application of the stain

to the glass is with a wash brush (Fig. 58), working it with a badger (Fig. 60) when wet. Stick lights may be introduced to add variety, while many other treatments may occur to the craftsman whilst he is experimenting.

Upon the adept use of silver stain in the right places often depends the success of the whole

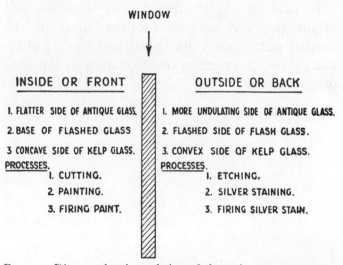

WINDOW

INSIDE OR FRONT	OUTSIDE OR BACK
1. FLATTER SIDE OF ANTIQUE GLASS.	1. MORE UNDULATING SIDE OF ANTIQUE GLASS.
2. BASE OF FLASHED GLASS	2. FLASHED SIDE OF FLASH GLASS.
3 CONCAVE SIDE OF KELP GLASS.	3. CONVEX SIDE OF KELP GLASS.

PROCESSES.

INSIDE OR FRONT	OUTSIDE OR BACK
1. CUTTING.	1. ETCHING.
2 PAINTING.	2. SILVER STAINING.
3. FIRING PAINT.	3. FIRING SILVER STAIN.

FIG. 71.—Diagram showing relation of the various processes to the two sides of the window.

window. Pale yellows and deep oranges may be obtained, and by careful handling a graduated range of these may be obtained on the same piece of glass. Some very brilliant effects may be obtained by using the stain in conjunction with white glass, but coloured glass will also take the stain. A specially prepared white flashed glass is made for staining and the extra cost is more than justified by the results. The glass is termed 'kelp' and in large sheets it will be seen that there is a slight curvature on the surface; it is the convex side which has been prepared for staining.

It is important to remember that flashed glass is always leaded up with the flashed side to the outside of the window, while it is the unflashed side that is cut.

In case any doubt should exist on which side of the glass any particular operation should be carried out, Fig. 71 has been included to summarize the processes in their relation to the sides of the window.

CHAPTER XI

FIRING

SUCCESSFUL firing can only be accomplished by practice. Each kiln requires different handling according to its special construction, but in every case the temperature should be raised slowly

FIG. 72.—Pressing glass on to powder on tray.

and after the required heat has been reached the glass should be cooled slowly.

The pieces of glass to be fired are placed on iron trays which are covered with some heat-resisting powder such as flint or plaster of Paris. Sufficient powder must be used to cover all the metal of the tray, and the surface of the powder

87

must be flat and smooth to provide a good mould for the glass.

The pieces of glass are placed on the powder with painted sides uppermost. Each piece must receive careful attention and be carefully pressed into position in the powder by holding the edges with the tips of the fingers and thumb in order to avoid contact of the hands with the paint (Fig. 72). The glass shapes may be moved backwards and forwards in an endeavour to

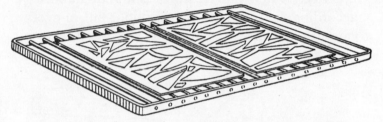

FIG. 73.—The rack with trays containing glass ready for the kiln.

press the powder quite flat and smooth underneath. Any air-hole enclosed in the mould may cause a break or mound to form in the glass during firing. Ridges or undulations in the surface of the powder may repeat themselves in the fired glass; a good method of levelling the powder is by use of a roller, or smoothing across with a knife blade. The edges of the pieces of glass should on no account touch each other on the tray, as if they are slightly overfired they may fuse and join together.

Having arranged the glass on the trays so that all the available space is occupied, the trays are now placed on an iron rack or grid ready for sliding into the kiln (Fig. 73).

Figs. 74 and 75 show the type of kiln suitable

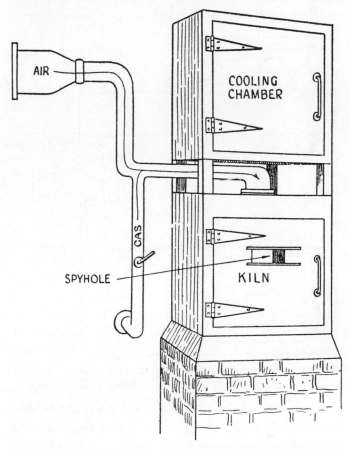

FIG. 74.—General sketch of kiln and cooling chamber.

for a school or small workshop. An electric fan provides a forced draught which combines with the gas to drive flames downwards from the honeycombed ceiling of the kiln on to the top of the glass in the trays.

First the gas is turned on and carefully lit. A match tied to the end of a long stick is a safe method of lighting the gas at the honeycomb.

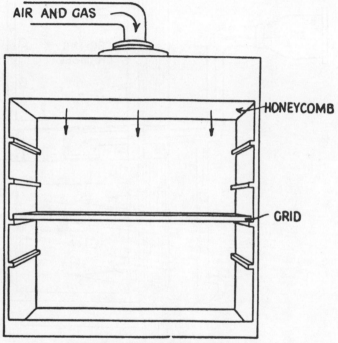

AIR AND GAS

HONEYCOMB

GRID

FIG. 75.—Interior of kiln.

The grid and trays are then slid into position and the draught switched on. The gas should be kept at about half pressure for a few minutes and then gradually increased at regular intervals for about fifteen or twenty minutes, when full pressure should be reached. A few minutes of firing at this temperature will fuse the pigment securely with the glass. A spy hole is usually provided for observation and through this the glass may be examined. At the point of fusing the top surface of the glass is molten and presents an appearance of wetness. Experience will enable one to recognize glass which has been just sufficiently fired.

The temperatures at which different types of glass will fuse with the paint vary, and the fusing point will also be affected by the varying ingredients of different pigments. Once the correct temperature height has been reached the draught and gas should be turned off and the glass left in the kiln to cool slowly. If more than two trays have to be fired the use of a cooling chamber (Fig. 74) is required. In this case the heat is turned off and the glass in the first two trays is allowed to cool slightly. The trays are then quickly withdrawn from the kiln, using a pair of asbestos gloves, and slid into the cooling chamber. The second pair of trays may now be placed in the kiln to warm up (a good plan is to warm the second pair of trays in the cooling oven while the first pair are being fired) and the heat turned on again.

The construction of the cooling oven is similar to that of the kiln except that it is not directly affected by heat. Its nearness to the kiln, sometimes on top and sometimes at the side, ensures sufficient hot air and fumes for safe cooling. The cooling glass must be sheltered from any draughts of cold air or the glass will crack. If the kiln will allow, several sets of trays may be placed in together, and as the top set reaches the required state of heat it should be removed to the cooling chamber and the next set moved up to the top.

To fire silver stain a lower temperature is required than for firing pigment. In addition to this it is the inside of the window that is painted and the outside that is stained. It is important therefore to see that the correct side of the glass is treated in each case and that the treated surface

FIG. 76.—Section showing glass packed for sending to fire.

must always be uppermost in the kiln during firing.

If the workshop or school combines pottery with stained glass work, the pottery kiln may be used to serve the purpose of a glass kiln, while large tins on or near the kiln may be used for cooling chambers. If the workshop cannot run to the expenditure required for a kiln the glass for firing must be carefully packed and sent to some convenient near-by kiln. The glass should be carefully and tightly packed flat in a wooden box between layers of cotton wool (Fig. 76). The box should be so packed as to prevent movement of the glass during transit which might cause breakage or disturb the pigment. Newspapers are useful as top and bottom packing and fill up space in a case only half full of glass.

Frying. Sometimes when painted glass has been fired it is found that the paint, instead of fusing flat into the glass, has dried into little bubbles which stand away from the surface of the glass and which can be rubbed off with the fingers. This disappointing feature is called 'frying', and when it occurs the dried bubbles must be rubbed away and the glass painted and fired again.

The cause of frying is mainly due to the paint being applied too thickly. Retouching paint before it has been fired also invariably results in frying. Should the paint appear too thin when it has dried, either wipe it off and repaint or fire it before retouching. Occasionally frying is caused by the presence of too much gum in the mixture. To obtain the best results the pigment should be well mixed and the glass fired as soon as possible after painting.

CHAPTER XII

FITTING A WINDOW

THIS work very often falls outside the scope of the craftsman in stained glass. The fitting of these windows, particularly if they are large, is a highly-skilled job requiring heavy labour and scaffolding.

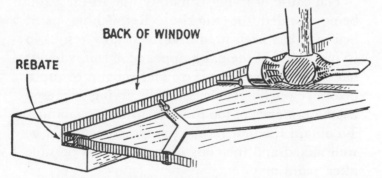

FIG. 77.—Showing method of fitting in wood frame.

It is well, however, that the craftsman appreciates the methods of fitting, especially in the case of small windows when he may be required to fit them himself.

The simplest method of fitting is to fix the window into a wooden frame and then fit the frame to the window space. The wooden frame, which should be rebated, is laid on the bench, and

94

the window placed in the rebate with the back (outside) uppermost. The window should be held in position by nails driven into the frame and left projecting a distance equal to the width of the outside calm. Care must be exercised when hammering to avoid cracking the glass; a useful precaution is to hammer along a lead line for safety (Fig. 77).

With small glass panels a frame may be used having grooves running all round the inside (Fig. 78). This holds the window very securely.

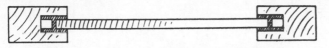

FIG. 78.—Fitting small panel with grooves in frame.

When a window is fitted directly to a stone window surround the usual method is to use a groove in conjunction with saddle bars. These are bars of iron, usually round in section, which run horizontally across the window at regular intervals up the window. They are very often used with sectional leaded windows, the bars coinciding with the section lines. Whatever the material for the window frame, it is drilled at the sides to take the ends of the crossing bars. One hole is bored to double the required depth so that the bar may be slid into position after the window is mounted (Fig. 79).

When two sections of a window have been mounted together (Chapter VII explains how this is done), the saddle bar is fitted and the

sections are wired together by twisting (Fig. 80).
After twisting the ends of the wire together the
ends should be nipped off with the pliers.

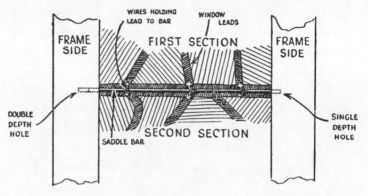

FIG. 79.—Showing a saddle bar fitted to a sectional window.

The method of grooving a window into a stone
frame is similar to the fitting of a saddle bar. One
groove is cut twice as deep as the other and this
enables the section to be manœuvred into
position. The lowest section is fitted first and the
others in rotation. A deeper groove is required at
the top of the frame in order to fit the top section,
though sometimes the section next to the top is
fitted last and the top two sections can be coaxed
into position without a specially deep groove at
the top.

Whatever the method of fitting, the process is
finished off by packing all cavities tightly with
cement and twisting all wires firmly so that the
window will be securely fixed and free from
vibration.

FITTING A WINDOW

Repairs. If a window has been well fitted and well made in all its processes, very little maintenance is necessary. Sometimes when a stained glass panel is fitted to a door the repeated vibration may loosen the leading. In this case the panel should be cemented again and the leads pressed back to the glass.

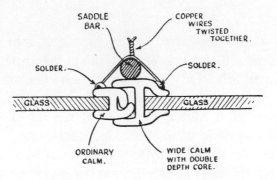

Fig. 80.—Section showing saddle bar holding sectional leaded window.

Should any one of the glass shapes get broken the surrounding lead flanges may be cut with the cutting knife and bent back to release the broken fragments. A paper or cardboard shape should be fitted to the opening and used as a template for cutting a fresh piece of glass. After fitting the new glass the flanges should be bent back, soldered and cemented.

CHAPTER XIII

SOME EXPERIMENTS WITH GLASS

1. **Glass Mosaics.** This provides some interesting panel work and at the same time uses up waste fragments of glass. In school work, for instance, students should keep their larger pieces of waste glass and at the end of periods of work or at intervals of waiting for tools, etc., they should cut the glass into small squares. These squares should be stored away in boxes or trays so that the various colours are separated and ready at any time for mosaic work.

It should be remembered that glass is translucent and that the colours of dark glass cannot be seen to advantage when light does not fall from the back and filter through. In mosaic work all light falls on the glass from the front and is reflected back, hence the background binding material should be as nearly white as possible in order to show off the colours to advantage. Plaster of Paris or silver crete cement are both very satisfactory for use with transparent glass, and when opaque glass is used ordinary bricklayers' cement will serve admirably.

The design for the mosaic should be formal and

depend upon two-dimensional pattern for interest. The small squares of glass are gummed face downwards on to the design with gum arabic (Fig. 81). It should be remembered that the

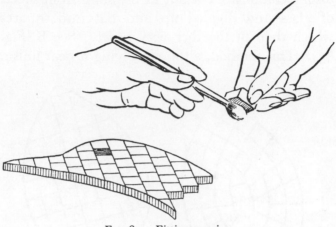

FIG. 81.—Fitting mosaics.

finished arrangement of the mosaic will be the reverse of the paper design. If a direct copy of the paper design is required a tracing must be made from the original and then turned over for working. The paper to which the squares of glass are gummed will slightly buckle as the pieces of glass are fixed in position (Fig. 82). Attempts are

FIG. 82.—Buckled paper giving variations.

sometimes made by mosaic workers to avoid this unevenness because it may at first appear to indicate faulty workmanship. Actually, however, the irregularity due to the buckle of the paper gives rise to sparkle and variety which greatly add to the interest of the panel.

To obtain a mosaic with a very neat finish there is another method. The areas that are all of one colour are cut out in the solid from sheets of glass and divided up and cut into squares which then fit together very neatly (See B, Fig. 83). This method, although giving a neat finish,

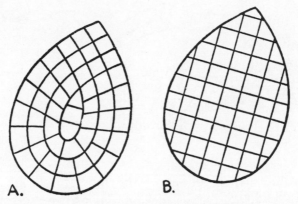

FIG. 83.—Two methods of breaking up shapes for mosaic.

does not use up waste material and detracts from the natural interest of mosaic, which lies in the slight variations of the colour of each square and in the irregular width of the cement lines in the finished mosaic.

(Note. The word 'cement' as used in this chapter must not be confused with the mixture used for sealing the joints of a window).

When all the pieces have been gummed in position, a wooden frame is fitted round the work. The frame is only temporary and need not be very strongly made, the depth will vary in relation to the area of the design.

The cement plaster is now added in two layers. The layer to be applied must be fairly thin so that it sinks into all the crevices between the glass squares and binds them together (Fig. 84). On

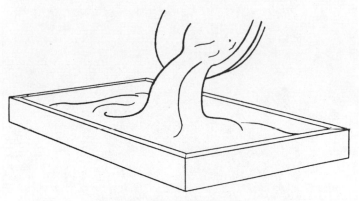

FIG. 84.—First layer of plaster.

this first layer may be placed thin laths, wire-netting, or sacking, to act as reinforcement to the cement. The second layer may be a little thicker and should be applied as quickly as possible after the first so that the layers combine securely.

When the plaster has set the paper may be peeled off from the front of the mosaic. If any difficulty is experienced in removing the paper it should be moistened with water and sponged off. Fig. 85 shows a completed mosaic panel.

The mosaic method of producing panel designs will quickly lead to many interesting experiments. The glass need not necessarily be cut into squares;

well-mixed plaster will hold irregular and larger shapes. If the glass is transparent, other materials such as coloured sand, string, and fragments of mirror, may be set in the plaster beneath the glass and these, by showing through the glass,

FIG. 85.—A mosaic panel.

will add variety to the mosaic. If larger pieces of glass are used, figures may be painted on the underside of the glass before cementing.

2. **Cement Windows.** This is a variation of window making in which no leads are necessary. Work of this type will be mainly without painting but there is no reason why the addition of pigment should not be attempted.

SOME EXPERIMENTS WITH GLASS

The cartoon is drawn but the design does not leave the usual lead spaces, instead greater space

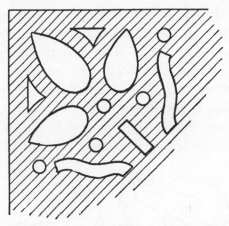

FIG. 86.—Type of pattern suitable for cement windows.

is allowed between the glass components (Fig. 86). The distance allowed between the glass

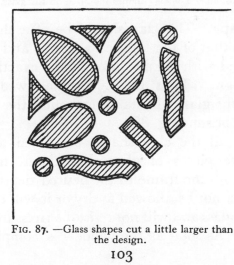

FIG. 87.—Glass shapes cut a little larger than the design.

shapes will depend upon the size of the window and the thickness of the cement. Unlike the leaded window very great accuracy is not demanded and the glass shapes should be cut $\frac{1}{4}''$ or so larger all round than the shapes shown on the design (Fig. 87). The design should be so arranged that reasonably wide strips of cement will separate the glass shapes even after the $\frac{1}{4}''$ overlap has been allowed for.

The glass shapes should now be mounted flat in a frame or box and a piece of clay placed on

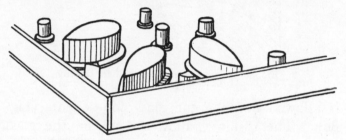

Fig. 88.—The clay shapes mounted on the glass.

each shape. The clay should be of a thickness equal to that of the finished window, and should be shaped with a knife to conform exactly with the design. Thus the overlap allowed when cutting the glass will stand out round the base of the clay prism (Fig. 88).

When all the clay shapes are fitted to their respective pieces of glass the cement may be poured into the frame to the desired depth. The clay must not be allowed to dry or it will cease to grip the glass and will not resist the pressure of the cement. As soon as the window is completed it should be fitted into a strong and permanent wooden frame, for the construction of these windows is delicate, especially if plaster of Paris is used as the cement. Fig. 89 shows the section of a finished window.

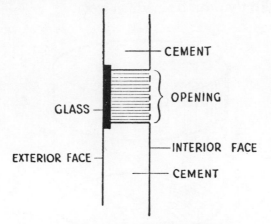

FIG. 89.—Section of cement window.

Windows made in this way are usually of simple, formal design and rely upon geometrical shapes to show a rich pattern of colour.

3. **Lamp Shades.** The making of lamp shades provides another variation of the combination of glass and light. Very narrow calm must be used or the total weight of the shade will make it impracticable. Shades made up by joining flat sections of leaded glass are comparatively simple and require no explanation. Spherical and cylindrical shades and other shapes including curved surfaces may cause some difficulty, however. A mould must first be made, over which to

105

build the shade. The mould should be made of wood or other material capable of holding nails when they are driven into it. Wood is the best material for these moulds because it can be easily turned to shape on a lathe. Fig. 90 shows some moulds that can be made in wood.

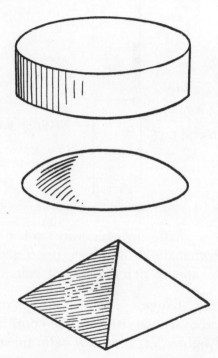

FIG. 90.—Wooden shapes for lamp shade making.

The glass and leads are built up together on the mould, starting at the most convenient place. For example, in a dome-shaped shade the best place to commence is in the centre, working from the top outwards and downwards, using nails

106

just as they are used for window making (Fig. 91).

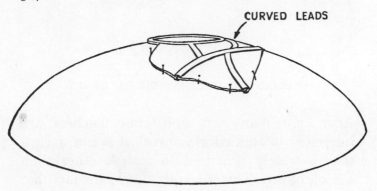

CURVED LEADS

FIG. 91.—Leading up a domed lamp shade.

These shades are soldered and cemented just the same as a window, while fittings for hanging the shade can be soldered to the outside lead rim.

CHAPTER XIV

STAINED GLASS AS A SCHOOL CRAFT

ALTHOUGH many art and craft teachers are interested in stained glass work it is not a craft that is widely practised in schools other than schools of art. This is largely due to the fact that work in stained glass is regarded as a forgotten craft and difficulties are magnified by a lack of understanding of the method of production of stained glass windows. Teachers who are convinced of the value of the craft will find it can be practised at no more expense than others of the school crafts. Firing is the chief difficulty, but, by using the school pottery kiln, if one exists, or sending the glass to a local school of art or works having a suitable kiln, the difficulty can be largely overcome.

Many teachers realize the value to the art course of practice in a medium through which light passes, in addition to the usual types of colour work where light falls on one side of the material and is reflected back. They often attempt to fulfil the need for this training by exercises in coloured paper of transparent and translucent qualities. Excellent as these and opaque coloured papers are they are useless and futile in themselves. The training in appreciation is positively detrimental because it neglects the beautiful qualities of the useful material, glass, and attempts to portray the brilliance of the features of a window in a useless material, paper. Work in glass the student can connect up with windows he sees about him; he will not see paper windows.

It is also a mistaken idea that the execution of a window or panel is beyond the capabilities of the average child. The work must, of course, be kept to simple shapes and processes, but the chief point to bear in mind is that the true character of glass must be appreciated.

After the first few shaky attempts boys and girls of senior and secondary school age will cut glass with confidence. If children are shown the correct methods and their work properly systematized, there will be little danger of cuts from the glass. The pleasure and excitement which children exhibit when matching pieces of glass, working out schemes of colour and leading, is in itself ample justification for the inclusion of this craft in the art scheme.

The work produced may be used in the school or the students may purchase their own. There are many windows in schools and homes which look out on to sordid or ugly scenes, and where the use of stained glass work can bring refreshing relief. The work naturally couples itself with pottery, and the field of mosaic work, both in the flat and the shaped, provides in itself enormous scope for school work under the direction of an alert art teacher.

General Suggestions for Classwork. The first exercise should consist of an introduction to the character of glass and the method of window construction. If the children begin by breaking up a rectangle by straight lines into simple shapes (Fig. 92) they will immediately be occupied by

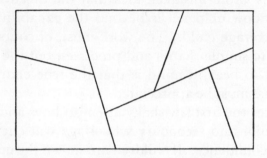

FIG. 92.—Rectangle broken up into simple shapes for an introductory exercise.

the processes of: 1, Cutline; 2, Glass cutting; 3, Leading up; 4, Soldering; 5, Cementing.

The second exercise should include painting from a prepared cartoon. The painting should be executed with the glass in a horizontal position so that the students realize to the full the necessity of working at an angle that will allow the paint to flow freely. The amount of leading for each student at this stage should be considered in relation to the ability shown by the first exercise. Some students may have difficulty with one process, some with another, and these facts should be noted for individual help to students and for influencing their future designs.

The glass used for this exercise in painting should be white, or at least transparent, so that no difficulty is experienced in the tracing process. This exercise need not necessarily include leading up, but this is a matter for the teacher to decide.

In the third exercise both painting and leading up should be combined in the production of a small panel suitable for hanging in front of a plain glass window by wire. The shapes must be kept simple, though good students at this stage may introduce curved lines into their designs. Rectangles, squares, lozenges, shields and circles provide a great variety of patterns and designs which make attractive glass panels.

By the time this third exercise is comple 1 the children should be capable of making small windows for requirements of their homes, of experimenting with scrap glass in the formation of mosaics, etc., and of working together in groups on community work. Sectional windows, by reason of their particular construction, are very suitable for group work. Great interest can be maintained in the design of large work by discussion and arrangement among the students themselves, who should all try to get some of their own ideas into the scheme. Community work must be well organized, and groups should have a responsible leader together with subordinate responsibilities given to each member, so that they realize the necessity of working together in harmony to produce harmonious work.

CHAPTER XV

EQUIPMENT, TOOLS AND MATERIALS

ANY room or part of a room can be adapted for the craft, though, for those who find little difficulty in obtaining their requirements, a high studio is recommended with plenty of light and window space. A set of racks for storing glass are necessary. In these the glass sheets should stand on edge with the various colours grouped together. The racks should be arranged so that the light falls from one side and the colour of the glass can easily be seen by pulling out the sheet an inch or two.

The cutting bench should be of a suitable height, and as pleasantly situated as possible, for much work has to be done on it.

Sets of drawers are useful for storing small pieces of glass, and trays should be kept containing supplies of mosaic squares.

A small separate room or part of the single room should be set aside for the dirtier work of leading up, soldering and cementing. Store places are required for leads and for acid (preferably a position in which the fumes are carried from the room). Provision must be made for some form of lead-vice and an acid bath. Lead keeps bright under sacking and will solder more easily. As large a variety of glass as possible should be kept for matching and patterning. Glass manufacturers supply sets of samples and these should be kept at hand for matching and ordering. A visit to a glass warehouse may be useful in order to examine various types of stock in large quantities, and it is a good plan to keep a record of materials, interesting experiments, and colour combinations, though the temptation to repeat successful designs must be overcome if there is to be progress.

Not all the articles set out below are necessary to make a start in the craft, many implements can be improvised and the beginner is advised to start by purchasing only the absolute necessities and adding to these as the scope of his work widens.

Tools, etc.:
    Bench for cutting, leading up, etc.
    Rack for storing glass.
    Window space to work at.
    Kiln and cooling oven.
    Sheet of plain glass for waxing up.
    Cutting knife for lead.
    Glass cutter.
    Glass worker's hammer.
    Brushes of various kinds, riggers, mops, badgers and
        scrubs.
    Palette and palette knife.
    Saucepan for wax.
    Stopping knife and lathekin.

Pliers.
Carpenter's hammer and nails.
Scrubbing brush for cement.
Laths and battens.
Oilstone.
File.
Soldering iron.
Easel.
Lead-vice.
Rags.

Materials:
A selection of glass. Cathedral, Flemish and other cheap glass to be used for exercises and simple work in the early stages of the craft. Antiques for window making. Flashed glass and staining glass.
Prepared glass paint.
Prepared silver stain.
Beeswax or plasticine for waxing up.
Leads—wide, medium and narrow calm.
Flux—Russian tallow in cylindrical sticks or killed spirits.
Soft solder in long narrow bars.
Ingredients for cement making.
Hydrofluoric acid stored in gutta-percha bottles.
Copper wire.
Resin.
Cartoon paper.

INDEX

A CATALOGUE OF SELECTED DOVER BOOKS
IN ALL FIELDS OF INTEREST

A CATALOGUE OF SELECTED DOVER BOOKS
IN ALL FIELDS OF INTEREST

AMERICA'S OLD MASTERS, James T. Flexner. Four men emerged unexpectedly from provincial 18th century America to leadership in European art: Benjamin West, J. S. Copley, C. R. Peale, Gilbert Stuart. Brilliant coverage of lives and contributions. Revised, 1967 edition. 69 plates. 365pp. of text.
21806-6 Paperbound $3.00

FIRST FLOWERS OF OUR WILDERNESS: AMERICAN PAINTING, THE COLONIAL PERIOD, James T. Flexner. Painters, and regional painting traditions from earliest Colonial times up to the emergence of Copley, West and Peale Sr., Foster, Gustavus Hesselius, Feke, John Smibert and many anonymous painters in the primitive manner. Engaging presentation, with 162 illustrations. xxii + 368pp.
22180-6 Paperbound $3.50

THE LIGHT OF DISTANT SKIES: AMERICAN PAINTING, 1760-1835, James T. Flexner. The great generation of early American painters goes to Europe to learn and to teach: West, Copley, Gilbert Stuart and others. Allston, Trumbull, Morse; also contemporary American painters—primitives, derivatives, academics—who remained in America. 102 illustrations. xiii + 306pp.
22179-2 Paperbound $3.50

A HISTORY OF THE RISE AND PROGRESS OF THE ARTS OF DESIGN IN THE UNITED STATES, William Dunlap. Much the richest mine of information on early American painters, sculptors, architects, engravers, miniaturists, etc. The only source of information for scores of artists, the major primary source for many others. Unabridged reprint of rare original 1834 edition, with new introduction by James T. Flexner, and 394 new illustrations. Edited by Rita Weiss. 6⅝ x 9⅝.
21695-0, 21696-9, 21697-7 Three volumes, Paperbound $15.00

EPOCHS OF CHINESE AND JAPANESE ART, Ernest F. Fenollosa. From primitive Chinese art to the 20th century, thorough history, explanation of every important art period and form, including Japanese woodcuts; main stress on China and Japan, but Tibet, Korea also included. Still unexcelled for its detailed, rich coverage of cultural background, aesthetic elements, diffusion studies, particularly of the historical period. 2nd, 1913 edition. 242 illustrations. lii + 439pp. of text.
20364-6, 20365-4 Two volumes, Paperbound $6.00

THE GENTLE ART OF MAKING ENEMIES, James A. M. Whistler. Greatest wit of his day deflates Oscar Wilde, Ruskin, Swinburne; strikes back at inane critics, exhibitions, art journalism; aesthetics of impressionist revolution in most striking form. Highly readable classic by great painter. Reproduction of edition designed by Whistler. Introduction by Alfred Werner. xxxvi + 334pp.
21875-9 Paperbound $3.00

VISUAL ILLUSIONS: THEIR CAUSES, CHARACTERISTICS, AND APPLICATIONS, Matthew Luckiesh. Thorough description and discussion of optical illusion, geometric and perspective, particularly; size and shape distortions, illusions of color, of motion; natural illusions; use of illusion in art and magic, industry, etc. Most useful today with op art, also for classical art. Scores of effects illustrated. Introduction by William H. Ittleson. 100 illustrations. xxi + 252pp.

21530-X Paperbound $2.00

A HANDBOOK OF ANATOMY FOR ART STUDENTS, Arthur Thomson. Thorough, virtually exhaustive coverage of skeletal structure, musculature, etc. Full text, supplemented by anatomical diagrams and drawings and by photographs of undraped figures. Unique in its comparison of male and female forms, pointing out differences of contour, texture, form. 211 figures, 40 drawings, 86 photographs. xx + 459pp. 5⅜ x 8⅜.

21163-0 Paperbound $3.50

150 MASTERPIECES OF DRAWING, Selected by Anthony Toney. Full page reproductions of drawings from the early 16th to the end of the 18th century, all beautifully reproduced: Rembrandt, Michelangelo, Dürer, Fragonard, Urs, Graf, Wouwerman, many others. First-rate browsing book, model book for artists. xviii + 150pp. 8⅜ x 11¼.

21032-4 Paperbound $2.50

THE LATER WORK OF AUBREY BEARDSLEY, Aubrey Beardsley. Exotic, erotic, ironic masterpieces in full maturity: Comedy Ballet, Venus and Tannhauser, Pierrot, Lysistrata, Rape of the Lock, Savoy material, Ali Baba, Volpone, etc. This material revolutionized the art world, and is still powerful, fresh, brilliant. With *The Early Work*, all Beardsley's finest work. 174 plates, 2 in color. xiv + 176pp. 8⅛ x 11.

21817-1 Paperbound $3.00

DRAWINGS OF REMBRANDT, Rembrandt van Rijn. Complete reproduction of fabulously rare edition by Lippmann and Hofstede de Groot, completely reedited, updated, improved by Prof. Seymour Slive, Fogg Museum. Portraits, Biblical sketches, landscapes, Oriental types, nudes, episodes from classical mythology—All Rembrandt's fertile genius. Also selection of drawings by his pupils and followers. "Stunning volumes," *Saturday Review*. 550 illustrations. lxxviii + 552pp. 9⅛ x 12¼.

21485-0, 21486-9 Two volumes, Paperbound $10.00

THE DISASTERS OF WAR, Francisco Goya. One of the masterpieces of Western civilization—83 etchings that record Goya's shattering, bitter reaction to the Napoleonic war that swept through Spain after the insurrection of 1808 and to war in general. Reprint of the first edition, with three additional plates from Boston's Museum of Fine Arts. All plates facsimile size. Introduction by Philip Hofer, Fogg Museum. v + 97pp. 9⅜ x 8¼.

21872-4 Paperbound $2.00

GRAPHIC WORKS OF ODILON REDON. Largest collection of Redon's graphic works ever assembled: 172 lithographs, 28 etchings and engravings, 9 drawings. These include some of his most famous works. All the plates from *Odilon Redon: oeuvre graphique complet,* plus additional plates. New introduction and caption translations by Alfred Werner. 209 illustrations. xxvii + 209pp. 9⅛ x 12¼.

21966-8 Paperbound $4.50

DESIGN BY ACCIDENT; A BOOK OF "ACCIDENTAL EFFECTS" FOR ARTISTS AND DESIGNERS, James F. O'Brien. Create your own unique, striking, imaginative effects by "controlled accident" interaction of materials: paints and lacquers, oil and water based paints, splatter, crackling materials, shatter, similar items. Everything you do will be different; first book on this limitless art, so useful to both fine artist and commercial artist. Full instructions. 192 plates showing "accidents," 8 in color. viii + 215pp. 8⅜ x 11¼. 21942-9 Paperbound $3.75

THE BOOK OF SIGNS, Rudolf Koch. Famed German type designer draws 493 beautiful symbols: religious, mystical, alchemical, imperial, property marks, runes, etc. Remarkable fusion of traditional and modern. Good for suggestions of timelessness, smartness, modernity. Text. vi + 104pp. 6⅛ x 9¼.
20162-7 Paperbound $1.25

HISTORY OF INDIAN AND INDONESIAN ART, Ananda K. Coomaraswamy. An unabridged republication of one of the finest books by a great scholar in Eastern art. Rich in descriptive material, history, social backgrounds; Sunga reliefs, Rajput paintings, Gupta temples, Burmese frescoes, textiles, jewelry, sculpture, etc. 400 photos. viii + 423pp. 6⅜ x 9¾. 21436-2 Paperbound $5.00

PRIMITIVE ART, Franz Boas. America's foremost anthropologist surveys textiles, ceramics, woodcarving, basketry, metalwork, etc.; patterns, technology, creation of symbols, style origins. All areas of world, but very full on Northwest Coast Indians. More than 350 illustrations of baskets, boxes, totem poles, weapons, etc. 378 pp.
20025-6 Paperbound $3.00

THE GENTLEMAN AND CABINET MAKER'S DIRECTOR, Thomas Chippendale. Full reprint (third edition, 1762) of most influential furniture book of all time, by master cabinetmaker. 200 plates, illustrating chairs, sofas, mirrors, tables, cabinets, plus 24 photographs of surviving pieces. Biographical introduction by N. Bienenstock. vi + 249pp. 9⅞ x 12¾. 21601-2 Paperbound $4.00

AMERICAN ANTIQUE FURNITURE, Edgar G. Miller, Jr. The basic coverage of all American furniture before 1840. Individual chapters cover type of furniture— clocks, tables, sideboards, etc.—chronologically, with inexhaustible wealth of data. More than 2100 photographs, all identified, commented on. Essential to all early American collectors. Introduction by H. E. Keyes. vi + 1106pp. 7⅞ x 10¾.
21599-7, 21600-4 Two volumes, Paperbound $11.00

PENNSYLVANIA DUTCH AMERICAN FOLK ART, Henry J. Kauffman. 279 photos, 28 drawings of tulipware, Fraktur script, painted tinware, toys, flowered furniture, quilts, samplers, hex signs, house interiors, etc. Full descriptive text. Excellent for tourist, rewarding for designer, collector. Map. 146pp. 7⅞ x 10¾.
21205-X Paperbound $2.50

EARLY NEW ENGLAND GRAVESTONE RUBBINGS, Edmund V. Gillon, Jr. 43 photographs, 226 carefully reproduced rubbings show heavily symbolic, sometimes macabre early gravestones, up to early 19th century. Remarkable early American primitive art, occasionally strikingly beautiful; always powerful. Text. xxvi + 207pp. 8⅜ x 11¼. 21380-3 Paperbound $3.50

ALPHABETS AND ORNAMENTS, Ernst Lehner. Well-known pictorial source for decorative alphabets, script examples, cartouches, frames, decorative title pages, calligraphic initials, borders, similar material. 14th to 19th century, mostly European. Useful in almost any graphic arts designing, varied styles. 750 illustrations. 256pp. 7 x 10.   21905-4 Paperbound $4.00

PAINTING: A CREATIVE APPROACH, Norman Colquhoun. For the beginner simple guide provides an instructive approach to painting: major stumbling blocks for beginner; overcoming them, technical points; paints and pigments; oil painting; watercolor and other media and color. New section on "plastic" paints. Glossary. Formerly *Paint Your Own Pictures*. 221pp.   22000-1 Paperbound $1.75

THE ENJOYMENT AND USE OF COLOR, Walter Sargent. Explanation of the relations between colors themselves and between colors in nature and art, including hundreds of little-known facts about color values, intensities, effects of high and low illumination, complementary colors. Many practical hints for painters, references to great masters. 7 color plates, 29 illustrations. x + 274pp.
20944-X Paperbound $2.75

THE NOTEBOOKS OF LEONARDO DA VINCI, compiled and edited by Jean Paul Richter. 1566 extracts from original manuscripts reveal the full range of Leonardo's versatile genius: all his writings on painting, sculpture, architecture, anatomy, astronomy, geography, topography, physiology, mining, music, etc., in both Italian and English, with 186 plates of manuscript pages and more than 500 additional drawings. Includes studies for the Last Supper, the lost Sforza monument, and other works. Total of xlvii + 866pp. 7⅞ x 10¾.
22572-0, 22573-9 Two volumes, Paperbound $11.00

MONTGOMERY WARD CATALOGUE OF 1895. Tea gowns, yards of flannel and pillow-case lace, stereoscopes, books of gospel hymns, the New Improved Singer Sewing Machine, side saddles, milk skimmers, straight-edged razors, high-button shoes, spittoons, and on and on . . . listing some 25,000 items, practically all illustrated. Essential to the shoppers of the 1890's, it is our truest record of the spirit of the period. Unaltered reprint of Issue No. 57, Spring and Summer 1895. Introduction by Boris Emmet. Innumerable illustrations. xiii + 624pp. 8½ x 11⅝.
22377-9 Paperbound $6.95

THE CRYSTAL PALACE EXHIBITION ILLUSTRATED CATALOGUE (LONDON, 1851). One of the wonders of the modern world—the Crystal Palace Exhibition in which all the nations of the civilized world exhibited their achievements in the arts and sciences—presented in an equally important illustrated catalogue. More than 1700 items pictured with accompanying text—ceramics, textiles, cast-iron work, carpets, pianos, sleds, razors, wall-papers, billiard tables, beehives, silverware and hundreds of other artifacts—represent the focal point of Victorian culture in the Western World. Probably the largest collection of Victorian decorative art ever assembled— indispensable for antiquarians and designers. Unabridged republication of the Art-Journal Catalogue of the Great Exhibition of 1851, with all terminal essays. New introduction by John Gloag, F.S.A. xxxiv + 426pp. 9 x 12.
22503-8 Paperbound $5.00

A History of Costume, Carl Köhler. Definitive history, based on surviving pieces of clothing primarily, and paintings, statues, etc. secondarily. Highly readable text, supplemented by 594 illustrations of costumes of the ancient Mediterranean peoples, Greece and Rome, the Teutonic prehistoric period; costumes of the Middle Ages, Renaissance, Baroque, 18th and 19th centuries. Clear, measured patterns are provided for many clothing articles. Approach is practical throughout. Enlarged by Emma von Sichart. 464pp. 21030-8 Paperbound $3.50.

Oriental Rugs, Antique and Modern, Walter A. Hawley. A complete and authoritative treatise on the Oriental rug—where they are made, by whom and how, designs and symbols, characteristics in detail of the six major groups, how to distinguish them and how to buy them. Detailed technical data is provided on periods, weaves, warps, wefts, textures, sides, ends and knots, although no technical background is required for an understanding. 11 color plates, 80 halftones, 4 maps. vi + 320pp. 6⅛ x 9⅛. 22366-3 Paperbound $5.00

Ten Books on Architecture, Vitruvius. By any standards the most important book on architecture ever written. Early Roman discussion of aesthetics of building, construction methods, orders, sites, and every other aspect of architecture has inspired, instructed architecture for about 2,000 years. Stands behind Palladio, Michelangelo, Bramante, Wren, countless others. Definitive Morris H. Morgan translation. 68 illustrations. xii + 331pp. 20645-9 Paperbound $3.00

The Four Books of Architecture, Andrea Palladio. Translated into every major Western European language in the two centuries following its publication in 1570, this has been one of the most influential books in the history of architecture. Complete reprint of the 1738 Isaac Ware edition. New introduction by Adolf Placzek, Columbia Univ. 216 plates. xxii + 110pp. of text. 9½ x 12¾. 21308-0 Clothbound $12.50

Sticks and Stones: A Study of American Architecture and Civilization, Lewis Mumford.One of the great classics of American cultural history. American architecture from the medieval-inspired earliest forms to the early 20th century; evolution of structure and style, and reciprocal influences on environment. 21 photographic illustrations. 238pp. 20202-X Paperbound $2.00

The American Builder's Companion, Asher Benjamin. The most widely used early 19th century architectural style and source book, for colonial up into Greek Revival periods. Extensive development of geometry of carpentering, construction of sashes, frames, doors, stairs; plans and elevations of domestic and other buildings. Hundreds of thousands of houses were built according to this book, now invaluable to historians, architects, restorers, etc. 1827 edition. 59 plates. 114pp. 7⅞ x 10¾. 22236-5 Paperbound $3.50

Dutch Houses in the Hudson Valley Before 1776, Helen Wilkinson Reynolds. The standard survey of the Dutch colonial house and outbuildings, with constructional features, decoration, and local history associated with individual homesteads. Introduction by Franklin D. Roosevelt. Map. 150 illustrations. 469pp. 6⅝ x 9¼. 21469-9 Paperbound $5.00

THE ARCHITECTURE OF COUNTRY HOUSES, Andrew J. Downing. Together with Vaux's *Villas and Cottages* this is the basic book for Hudson River Gothic architecture of the middle Victorian period. Full, sound discussions of general aspects of housing, architecture, style, decoration, furnishing, together with scores of detailed house plans, illustrations of specific buildings, accompanied by full text. Perhaps the most influential single American architectural book. 1850 edition. Introduction by J. Stewart Johnson. 321 figures, 34 architectural designs. xvi + 560pp.
22003-6 Paperbound $4.00

LOST EXAMPLES OF COLONIAL ARCHITECTURE, John Mead Howells. Full-page photographs of buildings that have disappeared or been so altered as to be denatured, including many designed by major early American architects. 245 plates. xvii + 248pp. 7⅞ x 10¾. 21143-6 Paperbound $3.50

DOMESTIC ARCHITECTURE OF THE AMERICAN COLONIES AND OF THE EARLY REPUBLIC, Fiske Kimball. Foremost architect and restorer of Williamsburg and Monticello covers nearly 200 homes between 1620-1825. Architectural details, construction, style features, special fixtures, floor plans, etc. Generally considered finest work in its area. 219 illustrations of houses, doorways, windows, capital mantels. xx + 314pp. 7⅞ x 10¾. 21743-4 Paperbound $4.00

EARLY AMERICAN ROOMS: 1650-1858, edited by Russell Hawes Kettell. Tour of 12 rooms, each representative of a different era in American history and each furnished, decorated, designed and occupied in the style of the era. 72 plans and elevations, 8-page color section, etc., show fabrics, wall papers, arrangements, etc. Full descriptive text. xvii + 200pp. of text. 8⅜ x 11¼.
21633-0 Paperbound $5.00

THE FITZWILLIAM VIRGINAL BOOK, edited by J. Fuller Maitland and W. B. Squire. Full modern printing of famous early 17th-century ms. volume of 300 works by Morley, Byrd, Bull, Gibbons, etc. For piano or other modern keyboard instrument; easy to read format. xxxvi + 938pp. 8⅜ x 11.
21068-5, 21069-3 Two volumes, Paperbound $10.00

KEYBOARD MUSIC, Johann Sebastian Bach. Bach Gesellschaft edition. A rich selection of Bach's masterpieces for the harpsichord: the six English Suites, six French Suites, the six Partitas (Clavierübung part I), the Goldberg Variations (Clavierübung part IV), the fifteen Two-Part Inventions and the fifteen Three-Part Sinfonias. Clearly reproduced on large sheets with ample margins; eminently playable. vi + 312pp. 8⅛ x 11. 22360-4 Paperbound $5.00

THE MUSIC OF BACH: AN INTRODUCTION, Charles Sanford Terry. A fine, nontechnical introduction to Bach's music, both instrumental and vocal. Covers organ music, chamber music, passion music, other types. Analyzes themes, developments, innovations. x + 114pp. 21075-8 Paperbound $1.50

BEETHOVEN AND HIS NINE SYMPHONIES, Sir George Grove. Noted British musicologist provides best history, analysis, commentary on symphonies. Very thorough, rigorously accurate; necessary to both advanced student and amateur music lover. 436 musical passages. vii + 407 pp. 20334-4 Paperbound $2.75

JOHANN SEBASTIAN BACH, Philipp Spitta. One of the great classics of musicology, this definitive analysis of Bach's music (and life) has never been surpassed. Lucid, nontechnical analyses of hundreds of pieces (30 pages devoted to St. Matthew Passion, 26 to B Minor Mass). Also includes major analysis of 18th-century music. 450 musical examples. 40-page musical supplement. Total of xx + 1799pp.

(EUK) 22278-0, 22279-9 Two volumes, Clothbound $17.50

MOZART AND HIS PIANO CONCERTOS, Cuthbert Girdlestone. The only full-length study of an important area of Mozart's creativity. Provides detailed analyses of all 23 concertos, traces inspirational sources. 417 musical examples. Second edition. 509pp. 21271-8 Paperbound $3.50

THE PERFECT WAGNERITE: A COMMENTARY ON THE NIBLUNG'S RING, George Bernard Shaw. Brilliant and still relevant criticism in remarkable essays on Wagner's Ring cycle, Shaw's ideas on political and social ideology behind the plots, role of Leitmotifs, vocal requisites, etc. Prefaces. xxi + 136pp.

(USO) 21707-8 Paperbound $1.75

DON GIOVANNI, W. A. Mozart. Complete libretto, modern English translation; biographies of composer and librettist; accounts of early performances and critical reaction. Lavishly illustrated. All the material you need to understand and appreciate this great work. Dover Opera Guide and Libretto Series; translated and introduced by Ellen Bleiler. 92 illustrations. 209pp.

21134-7 Paperbound $2.00

BASIC ELECTRICITY, U. S. Bureau of Naval Personel. Originally a training course, best non-technical coverage of basic theory of electricity and its applications. Fundamental concepts, batteries, circuits, conductors and wiring techniques, AC and DC, inductance and capacitance, generators, motors, transformers, magnetic amplifiers, synchros, servomechanisms, etc. Also covers blue-prints, electrical diagrams, etc. Many questions, with answers. 349 illustrations. x + 448pp. 6½ x 9¼.

20973-3 Paperbound $3.50

REPRODUCTION OF SOUND, Edgar Villchur. Thorough coverage for laymen of high fidelity systems, reproducing systems in general, needles, amplifiers, preamps, loudspeakers, feedback, explaining physical background. "A rare talent for making technicalities vividly comprehensible," R. Darrell, *High Fidelity*. 69 figures. iv + 92pp. 21515-6 Paperbound $1.35

HEAR ME TALKIN' TO YA: THE STORY OF JAZZ AS TOLD BY THE MEN WHO MADE IT, Nat Shapiro and Nat Hentoff. Louis Armstrong, Fats Waller, Jo Jones, Clarence Williams, Billy Holiday, Duke Ellington, Jelly Roll Morton and dozens of other jazz greats tell how it was in Chicago's South Side, New Orleans, depression Harlem and the modern West Coast as jazz was born and grew. xvi + 429pp.

21726-4 Paperbound $3.00

FABLES OF AESOP, translated by Sir Roger L'Estrange. A reproduction of the very rare 1931 Paris edition; a selection of the most interesting fables, together with 50 imaginative drawings by Alexander Calder. v + 128pp. 6½x9¼.

21780-9 Paperbound $1.50

AGAINST THE GRAIN (A REBOURS), Joris K. Huysmans. Filled with weird images, evidences of a bizarre imagination, exotic experiments with hallucinatory drugs, rich tastes and smells and the diversions of its sybarite hero Duc Jean des Esseintes, this classic novel pushed 19th-century literary decadence to its limits. Full unabridged edition. Do not confuse this with abridged editions generally sold. Introduction by Havelock Ellis. xlix + 206pp. 22190-3 Paperbound $2.50

VARIORUM SHAKESPEARE: HAMLET. Edited by Horace H. Furness; a landmark of American scholarship. Exhaustive footnotes and appendices treat all doubtful words and phrases, as well as suggested critical emendations throughout the play's history. First volume contains editor's own text, collated with all Quartos and Folios. Second volume contains full first Quarto, translations of Shakespeare's sources (Belleforest, and Saxo Grammaticus), Der Bestrafte Brudermord, and many essays on critical and historical points of interest by major authorities of past and present. Includes details of staging and costuming over the years. By far the best edition available for serious students of Shakespeare. Total of xx + 905pp.
21004-9, 21005-7, 2 volumes, Paperbound $7.00

A LIFE OF WILLIAM SHAKESPEARE, Sir Sidney Lee. This is the standard life of Shakespeare, summarizing everything known about Shakespeare and his plays. Incredibly rich in material, broad in coverage, clear and judicious, it has served thousands as the best introduction to Shakespeare. 1931 edition. 9 plates. xxix + 792pp. 21967-4 Paperbound $3.75

MASTERS OF THE DRAMA, John Gassner. Most comprehensive history of the drama in print, covering every tradition from Greeks to modern Europe and America, including India, Far East, etc. Covers more than 800 dramatists, 2000 plays, with biographical material, plot summaries, theatre history, criticism, etc. "Best of its kind in English," *New Republic*. 77 illustrations. xxii + 890pp.
20100-7 Clothbound $10.00

THE EVOLUTION OF THE ENGLISH LANGUAGE, George McKnight. The growth of English, from the 14th century to the present. Unusual, non-technical account presents basic information in very interesting form: sound shifts, change in grammar and syntax, vocabulary growth, similar topics. Abundantly illustrated with quotations. Formerly *Modern English in the Making*. xii + 590pp.
21932-1 Paperbound $3.50

AN ETYMOLOGICAL DICTIONARY OF MODERN ENGLISH, Ernest Weekley. Fullest, richest work of its sort, by foremost British lexicographer. Detailed word histories, including many colloquial and archaic words; extensive quotations. Do not confuse this with the Concise Etymological Dictionary, which is much abridged. Total of xxvii + 830pp. 6½ x 9¼.
21873-2, 21874-0 Two volumes, Paperbound $7.90

FLATLAND: A ROMANCE OF MANY DIMENSIONS, E. A. Abbott. Classic of science-fiction explores ramifications of life in a two-dimensional world, and what happens when a three-dimensional being intrudes. Amusing reading, but also useful as introduction to thought about hyperspace. Introduction by Banesh Hoffmann. 16 illustrations. xx + 103pp. 20001-9 Paperbound $1.00

POEMS OF ANNE BRADSTREET, edited with an introduction by Robert Hutchinson. A new selection of poems by America's first poet and perhaps the first significant woman poet in the English language. 48 poems display her development in works of considerable variety—love poems, domestic poems, religious meditations, formal elegies, "quaternions," etc. Notes, bibliography. viii + 222pp.
22160-1 Paperbound $2.50

THREE GOTHIC NOVELS: THE CASTLE OF OTRANTO BY HORACE WALPOLE; VATHEK BY WILLIAM BECKFORD; THE VAMPYRE BY JOHN POLIDORI, WITH FRAGMENT OF A NOVEL BY LORD BYRON, edited by E. F. Bleiler. The first Gothic novel, by Walpole; the finest Oriental tale in English, by Beckford; powerful Romantic supernatural story in versions by Polidori and Byron. All extremely important in history of literature; all still exciting, packed with supernatural thrills, ghosts, haunted castles, magic, etc. xl + 291pp.
21232-7 Paperbound $2.50

THE BEST TALES OF HOFFMANN, E. T. A. Hoffmann. 10 of Hoffmann's most important stories, in modern re-editings of standard translations: Nutcracker and the King of Mice, Signor Formica, Automata, The Sandman, Rath Krespel, The Golden Flowerpot, Master Martin the Cooper, The Mines of Falun, The King's Betrothed, A New Year's Eve Adventure. 7 illustrations by Hoffmann. Edited by E. F. Bleiler. xxxix + 419pp.
21793-0 Paperbound $3.00

GHOST AND HORROR STORIES OF AMBROSE BIERCE, Ambrose Bierce. 23 strikingly modern stories of the horrors latent in the human mind: The Eyes of the Panther, The Damned Thing, An Occurrence at Owl Creek Bridge, An Inhabitant of Carcosa, etc., plus the dream-essay, Visions of the Night. Edited by E. F. Bleiler. xxii + 199pp.
20767-6 Paperbound $1.50

BEST GHOST STORIES OF J. S. LEFANU, J. Sheridan LeFanu. Finest stories by Victorian master often considered greatest supernatural writer of all. Carmilla, Green Tea, The Haunted Baronet, The Familiar, and 12 others. Most never before available in the U. S. A. Edited by E. F. Bleiler. 8 illustrations from Victorian publications. xvii + 467pp.
20415-4 Paperbound $3.00

MATHEMATICAL FOUNDATIONS OF INFORMATION THEORY, A. I. Khinchin. Comprehensive introduction to work of Shannon, McMillan, Feinstein and Khinchin, placing these investigations on a rigorous mathematical basis. Covers entropy concept in probability theory, uniqueness theorem, Shannon's inequality, ergodic sources, the E property, martingale concept, noise, Feinstein's fundamental lemma, Shanon's first and second theorems. Translated by R. A. Silverman and M. D. Friedman. iii + 120pp.
60434-9 Paperbound $2.00

SEVEN SCIENCE FICTION NOVELS, H. G. Wells. The standard collection of the great novels. Complete, unabridged. *First Men in the Moon, Island of Dr. Moreau, War of the Worlds, Food of the Gods, Invisible Man, Time Machine, In the Days of the Comet.* Not only science fiction fans, but every educated person owes it to himself to read these novels. 1015pp. (USO) 20264-X Clothbound $6.00

LAST AND FIRST MEN AND STAR MAKER, TWO SCIENCE FICTION NOVELS, Olaf Stapledon. Greatest future histories in science fiction. In the first, human intelligence is the "hero," through strange paths of evolution, interplanetary invasions, incredible technologies, near extinctions and reemergences. Star Maker describes the quest of a band of star rovers for intelligence itself, through time and space: weird inhuman civilizations, crustacean minds, symbiotic worlds, etc. Complete, unabridged. v + 438pp. (USO) 21962-3 Paperbound $2.50

THREE PROPHETIC NOVELS, H. G. WELLS. Stages of a consistently planned future for mankind. *When the Sleeper Wakes,* and *A Story of the Days to Come,* anticipate *Brave New World* and *1984,* in the 21st Century; *The Time Machine,* only complete version in print, shows farther future and the end of mankind. All show Wells's greatest gifts as storyteller and novelist. Edited by E. F. Bleiler. x + 335pp. (USO) 20605-X Paperbound $2.50

THE DEVIL'S DICTIONARY, Ambrose Bierce. America's own Oscar Wilde— Ambrose Bierce—offers his barbed iconoclastic wisdom in over 1,000 definitions hailed by H. L. Mencken as "some of the most gorgeous witticisms in the English language." 145pp. 20487-1 Paperbound $1.25

MAX AND MORITZ, Wilhelm Busch. Great children's classic, father of comic strip, of two bad boys, Max and Moritz. Also Ker and Plunk (Plisch und Plumm), Cat and Mouse, Deceitful Henry, Ice-Peter, The Boy and the Pipe, and five other pieces. Original German, with English translation. Edited by H. Arthur Klein; translations by various hands and H. Arthur Klein. vi + 216pp. 20181-3 Paperbound $2.00

PIGS IS PIGS AND OTHER FAVORITES, Ellis Parker Butler. The title story is one of the best humor short stories, as Mike Flannery obfuscates biology and English. Also included, That Pup of Murchison's, The Great American Pie Company, and Perkins of Portland. 14 illustrations. v + 109pp. 21532-6 Paperbound $1.25

THE PETERKIN PAPERS, Lucretia P. Hale. It takes genius to be as stupidly mad as the Peterkins, as they decide to become wise, celebrate the "Fourth," keep a cow, and otherwise strain the resources of the Lady from Philadelphia. Basic book of American humor. 153 illustrations. 219pp. 20794-3 Paperbound $2.00

PERRAULT'S FAIRY TALES, translated by A. E. Johnson and S. R. Littlewood, with 34 full-page illustrations by Gustave Doré. All the original Perrault stories— Cinderella, Sleeping Beauty, Bluebeard, Little Red Riding Hood, Puss in Boots, Tom Thumb, etc.—with their witty verse morals and the magnificent illustrations of Doré. One of the five or six great books of European fairy tales. viii + 117pp. 8⅛ x 11. 22311-6 Paperbound $2.00

OLD HUNGARIAN FAIRY TALES, Baroness Orczy. Favorites translated and adapted by author of the *Scarlet Pimpernel.* Eight fairy tales include "The Suitors of Princess Fire-Fly," "The Twin Hunchbacks," "Mr. Cuttlefish's Love Story," and "The Enchanted Cat." This little volume of magic and adventure will captivate children as it has for generations. 90 drawings by Montagu Barstow. 96pp. (USO) 22293-4 Paperbound $1.95

THE RED FAIRY BOOK, Andrew Lang. Lang's color fairy books have long been children's favorites. This volume includes Rapunzel, Jack and the Bean-stalk and 35 other stories, familiar and unfamiliar. 4 plates, 93 illustrations x + 367pp.
21673-X Paperbound $2.50

THE BLUE FAIRY BOOK, Andrew Lang. Lang's tales come from all countries and all times. Here are 37 tales from Grimm, the Arabian Nights, Greek Mythology, and other fascinating sources. 8 plates, 130 illustrations. xi + 390pp.
21437-0 Paperbound $2.50

HOUSEHOLD STORIES BY THE BROTHERS GRIMM. Classic English-language edition of the well-known tales — Rumpelstiltskin, Snow White, Hansel and Gretel, The Twelve Brothers, Faithful John, Rapunzel, Tom Thumb (52 stories in all). Translated into simple, straightforward English by Lucy Crane. Ornamented with headpieces, vignettes, elaborate decorative initials and a dozen full-page illustrations by Walter Crane. x + 269pp.
21080-4 Paperbound **$2.00**

THE MERRY ADVENTURES OF ROBIN HOOD, Howard Pyle. The finest modern versions of the traditional ballads and tales about the great English outlaw. Howard Pyle's complete prose version, with every word, every illustration of the first edition. Do not confuse this facsimile of the original (1883) with modern editions that change text or illustrations. 23 plates plus many page decorations. xxii + 296pp.
22043-5 Paperbound $2.50

THE STORY OF KING ARTHUR AND HIS KNIGHTS, Howard Pyle. The finest children's version of the life of King Arthur; brilliantly retold by Pyle, with 48 of his most imaginative illustrations. xviii + 313pp. 6⅛ x 9¼.
21445-1 Paperbound $2.50

THE WONDERFUL WIZARD OF OZ, L. Frank Baum. America's finest children's book in facsimile of first edition with all Denslow illustrations in full color. The edition a child should have. Introduction by Martin Gardner. 23 color plates, scores of drawings. iv + 267pp.
20691-2 Paperbound $2.50

THE MARVELOUS LAND OF OZ, L. Frank Baum. The second Oz book, every bit as imaginative as the Wizard. The hero is a boy named Tip, but the Scarecrow and the Tin Woodman are back, as is the Oz magic. 16 color plates, 120 drawings by John R. Neill. 287pp.
20692-0 Paperbound $2.50

THE MAGICAL MONARCH OF MO, L. Frank Baum. Remarkable adventures in a land even stranger than Oz. The best of Baum's books not in the Oz series. 15 color plates and dozens of drawings by Frank Verbeck. xviii + 237pp.
21892-9 Paperbound $2.25

THE BAD CHILD'S BOOK OF BEASTS, MORE BEASTS FOR WORSE CHILDREN, A MORAL ALPHABET, Hilaire Belloc. Three complete humor classics in one volume. Be kind to the frog, and do not call him names . . . and 28 other whimsical animals. Familiar favorites and some not so well known. Illustrated by Basil Blackwell. 156pp.
(USO) 20749-8 Paperbound $1.50

EAST O' THE SUN AND WEST O' THE MOON, George W. Dasent. Considered the best of all translations of these Norwegian folk tales, this collection has been enjoyed by generations of children (and folklorists too). Includes True and Untrue, Why the Sea is Salt, East O' the Sun and West O' the Moon, Why the Bear is Stumpy-Tailed, Boots and the Troll, The Cock and the Hen, Rich Peter the Pedlar, and 52 more. The only edition with all 59 tales. 77 illustrations by Erik Werenskiold and Theodor Kittelsen. xv + 418pp. 22521-6 Paperbound $3.50

GOOPS AND HOW TO BE THEM, Gelett Burgess. Classic of tongue-in-cheek humor, masquerading as etiquette book. 87 verses, twice as many cartoons, show mischievous Goops as they demonstrate to children virtues of table manners, neatness, courtesy, etc. Favorite for generations. viii + 88pp. 6½ x 9¼. 22233-0 Paperbound $1.25

ALICE'S ADVENTURES UNDER GROUND, Lewis Carroll. The first version, quite different from the final Alice in Wonderland, printed out by Carroll himself with his own illustrations. Complete facsimile of the "million dollar" manuscript Carroll gave to Alice Liddell in 1864. Introduction by Martin Gardner. viii + 96pp. Title and dedication pages in color. 21482-6 Paperbound $1.25

THE BROWNIES, THEIR BOOK, Palmer Cox. Small as mice, cunning as foxes, exuberant and full of mischief, the Brownies go to the zoo, toy shop, seashore, circus, etc., in 24 verse adventures and 266 illustrations. Long a favorite, since their first appearance in St. Nicholas Magazine. xi + 144pp. 6⅝ x 9¼. 21265-3 Paperbound $1.75

SONGS OF CHILDHOOD, Walter De La Mare. Published (under the pseudonym Walter Ramal) when De La Mare was only 29, this charming collection has long been a favorite children's book. A facsimile of the first edition in paper, the 47 poems capture the simplicity of the nursery rhyme and the ballad, including such lyrics as I Met Eve, Tartary, The Silver Penny. vii + 106pp. (USO) 21972-0 Paperbound $1.25

THE COMPLETE NONSENSE OF EDWARD LEAR, Edward Lear. The finest 19th-century humorist-cartoonist in full: all nonsense limericks, zany alphabets, Owl and Pussycat, songs, nonsense botany, and more than 500 illustrations by Lear himself. Edited by Holbrook Jackson. xxix + 287pp. (USO) 20167-8 Paperbound $2.00

BILLY WHISKERS: THE AUTOBIOGRAPHY OF A GOAT, Frances Trego Montgomery. A favorite of children since the early 20th century, here are the escapades of that rambunctious, irresistible and mischievous goat—Billy Whiskers. Much in the spirit of Peck's Bad Boy, this is a book that children never tire of reading or hearing. All the original familiar illustrations by W. H. Fry are included: 6 color plates, 18 black and white drawings. 159pp. 22345-0 Paperbound $2.00

MOTHER GOOSE MELODIES. Faithful republication of the fabulously rare Munroe and Francis "copyright 1833" Boston edition—the most important Mother Goose collection, usually referred to as the "original." Familiar rhymes plus many rare ones, with wonderful old woodcut illustrations. Edited by E. F. Bleiler. 128pp. 4½ x 6⅜. 22577-1 Paperbound $1.00

TWO LITTLE SAVAGES; BEING THE ADVENTURES OF TWO BOYS WHO LIVED AS INDIANS AND WHAT THEY LEARNED, Ernest Thompson Seton. Great classic of nature and boyhood provides a vast range of woodlore in most palatable form, a genuinely entertaining story. Two farm boys build a teepee in woods and live in it for a month, working out Indian solutions to living problems, star lore, birds and animals, plants, etc. 293 illustrations. vii + 286pp.
20985-7 Paperbound $2.50

PETER PIPER'S PRACTICAL PRINCIPLES OF PLAIN & PERFECT PRONUNCIATION. Alliterative jingles and tongue-twisters of surprising charm, that made their first appearance in America about 1830. Republished in full with the spirited woodcut illustrations from this earliest American edition. 32pp. $4\frac{1}{2}$ x $6\frac{3}{8}$.
22560-7 Paperbound $1.00

SCIENCE EXPERIMENTS AND AMUSEMENTS FOR CHILDREN, Charles Vivian. 73 easy experiments, requiring only materials found at home or easily available, such as candles, coins, steel wool, etc.; illustrate basic phenomena like vacuum, simple chemical reaction, etc. All safe. Modern, well-planned. Formerly *Science Games for Children*. 102 photos, numerous drawings. 96pp. $6\frac{1}{8}$ x $9\frac{1}{4}$.
21856-2 Paperbound $1.25

AN INTRODUCTION TO CHESS MOVES AND TACTICS SIMPLY EXPLAINED, Leonard Barden. Informal intermediate introduction, quite strong in explaining reasons for moves. Covers basic material, tactics, important openings, traps, positional play in middle game, end game. Attempts to isolate patterns and recurrent configurations. Formerly *Chess*. 58 figures. 102pp. (USO) 21210-6 Paperbound $1.25

LASKER'S MANUAL OF CHESS, Dr. Emanuel Lasker. Lasker was not only one of the five great World Champions, he was also one of the ablest expositors, theorists, and analysts. In many ways, his Manual, permeated with his philosophy of battle, filled with keen insights, is one of the greatest works ever written on chess. Filled with analyzed games by the great players. A single-volume library that will profit almost any chess player, beginner or master. 308 diagrams. xli x 349pp.
20640-8 Paperbound $2.75

THE MASTER BOOK OF MATHEMATICAL RECREATIONS, Fred Schuh. In opinion of many the finest work ever prepared on mathematical puzzles, stunts, recreations; exhaustively thorough explanations of mathematics involved, analysis of effects, citation of puzzles and games. Mathematics involved is elementary. Translated bv F. Göbel. 194 figures. xxiv + 430pp.
22134-2 Paperbound $3.50

MATHEMATICS, MAGIC AND MYSTERY, Martin Gardner. Puzzle editor for Scientific American explains mathematics behind various mystifying tricks: card tricks, stage "mind reading," coin and match tricks, counting out games, geometric dissections, etc. Probability sets, theory of numbers clearly explained. Also provides more than 400 tricks, guaranteed to work, that you can do. 135 illustrations. xii + 176pp.
20335-2 Paperbound $1.75

MATHEMATICAL PUZZLES FOR BEGINNERS AND ENTHUSIASTS, Geoffrey Mott-Smith. 189 puzzles from easy to difficult—involving arithmetic, logic, algebra, properties of digits, probability, etc.—for enjoyment and mental stimulus. Explanation of mathematical principles behind the puzzles. 135 illustrations. viii + 248pp.
20198-8 Paperbound $1.75

PAPER FOLDING FOR BEGINNERS, William D. Murray and Francis J. Rigney. Easiest book on the market, clearest instructions on making interesting, beautiful origami. Sail boats, cups, roosters, frogs that move legs, bonbon boxes, standing birds, etc. 40 projects; more than 275 diagrams and photographs. 94pp.
20713-7 Paperbound $1.00

TRICKS AND GAMES ON THE POOL TABLE, Fred Herrmann. 79 tricks and games— some solitaires, some for two or more players, some competitive games—to entertain you between formal games. Mystifying shots and throws, unusual caroms, tricks involving such props as cork, coins, a hat, etc. Formerly *Fun on the Pool Table*. 77 figures. 95pp.
21814-7 Paperbound $1.25

HAND SHADOWS TO BE THROWN UPON THE WALL: A SERIES OF NOVEL AND AMUSING FIGURES FORMED BY THE HAND, Henry Bursill. Delightful picturebook from great-grandfather's day shows how to make 18 different hand shadows: a bird that flies, duck that quacks, dog that wags his tail, camel, goose, deer, boy, turtle, etc. Only book of its sort. vi + 33pp. 6½ x 9¼. 21779-5 Paperbound $1.00

WHITTLING AND WOODCARVING, E. J. Tangerman. 18th printing of best book on market. "If you can cut a potato you can carve" toys and puzzles, chains, chessmen, caricatures, masks, frames, woodcut blocks, surface patterns, much more. Information on tools, woods, techniques. Also goes into serious wood sculpture from Middle Ages to present, East and West. 464 photos, figures. x + 293pp.
20965-2 Paperbound $2.00

HISTORY OF PHILOSOPHY, Julián Marias. Possibly the clearest, most easily followed, best planned, most useful one-volume history of philosophy on the market; neither skimpy nor overfull. Full details on system of every major philosopher and dozens of less important thinkers from pre-Socratics up to Existentialism and later. Strong on many European figures usually omitted. Has gone through dozens of editions in Europe. 1966 edition, translated by Stanley Appelbaum and Clarence Strowbridge. xviii + 505pp. 21739-6 Paperbound $3.50

YOGA: A SCIENTIFIC EVALUATION, Kovoor T. Behanan. Scientific but non-technical study of physiological results of yoga exercises; done under auspices of Yale U. Relations to Indian thought, to psychoanalysis, etc. 16 photos. xxiii + 270pp.
20505-3 Paperbound $2.50

Prices subject to change without notice.
Available at your book dealer or write for free catalogue to Dept. GI, Dover Publications, Inc., 180 Varick St., N. Y., N. Y. 10014. Dover publishes more than 150 books each year on science, elementary and advanced mathematics, biology, music, art, literary history, social sciences and other areas.